OAK KNOLL SERIES
on
THE HISTORY OF THE BOOK

Previous Volumes in the
OAK KNOLL SERIES
on
THE HISTORY OF THE BOOK

Volume I
THE ART OF BOOK-BINDING
by Edward Walker
With an Introduction
by Paul S. Koda

Volume II
THE PRINTER'S COMPOSITION MATRIX
by Richard E. Huss

Volume III
THE MAKING OF THE BOOK
by Alfred J. Cox
With an Introduction
by Paul S. Koda

Volume IV
THE BIOGRAPHY OF OTTMAR MERGENTHALER
Edited by Carl Schlesinger
With an introduction
by Elizabeth Harris

ANNALS OF
AMERICAN BOOKSELLING

ANNALS OF AMERICAN BOOKSELLING 1638-1850

HENRY WALCOTT BOYNTON

WITH AN INTRODUCTION BY
JOSEPH ROSENBLUM

NEW CASTLE
OAK KNOLL BOOKS
1991

FIRST PUBLISHED IN 1932
REPRINTED IN 1991 BY OAK KNOLL BOOKS,
414 DELAWARE STREET, NEW CASTLE, DE 19720
INTRODUCTION COPYRIGHT © 1991 JOSEPH ROSENBLUM
PRINTED IN THE UNITED STATES OF AMERICA

LIBRARY OF CONGRESS CATALOGING-IN-PUBLICATION DATA
Boynton, Henry Walcott, 1869-1947.
   Annals of American bookselling, 1638-1850 / by Henry Walcott
Boynton ; with an introduction by Joseph Rosenblum.
       p.   cm. — (Oak Knoll series on the history of the book)
   Reprint. Originally published: New York : Wiley, 1932.
   Includes bibliographical references (p.   ) and index.
   ISBN 0-938768-25-5
   1. Booksellers and bookselling—United States—History. 2. Book
industries and trade—United States—History. I. Title. II. Series.
Z473.B79   1991
381'.45002'0973—dc20
                                                       91-7156
                                                         CIP

INTRODUCTION

HENRY WALCOTT BOYNTON's book first appeared in 1932 to celebrate the 125th anniversary of its publisher, John Wiley and Sons, which had been started by Charles Wiley in 1807. In some ways its title is misleading—the volume does not offer a precise chronology; it focuses on publishers and printers more than on those who just sold books; and its America is limited to the eastern seaboard, especially Boston, New York and Philadelphia. Even within these limits Boynton did not seek comprehensiveness; as he wrote in his preface, his interest lay in the colorful figures that populated the book world of early America. Still, he tells a fascinating story in an entertaining manner.

Boynton's account begins, as it should, with the establishment of the Cambridge Press in Massachusetts Bay in 1638. For March 1639 John Winthrop wrote in his journal, "A printing house was begun at Cambridge by one Daye, at the charge of Mr. Glover, who died on seas hitherward. The first thing which was printed was the freeman's oath; the next was an almanac made for New England by Mr. William Peirce, Mariner; the next was the Psalms newly turned into metre" (Winship 1945, 1). No copy survives of the first two items, leaving what is commonly known as *The Bay Psalm Book* as the Gutenberg Bible of the United States. Translated in 1637-38 by three Massachusetts divines (Richard Mather, Thomas Welde and John Eliot), perhaps with some assistance from the

Introduction

Englishman Francis Quarles of emblem book fame, the volume appeared in an edition of 1,700 copies in 1640; of these, eleven survive. Though it is thus much scarcer than the Gutenberg Bible itself, it is more common than many other of the approximately two hundred publications that came from the Cambridge Press between 1638 and 1692, when the press ceased operation in Massachusetts. About forty of its imprints no longer survive, and many others exist in unique copies. The printing press itself fared better than its products, migrating to Vermont to create that state's first imprint. The press now rests in the Vermont Historical Society.

Boynton credits Stephe Day(e), Sr., with being the first printer in British North America, a century after Juan Pablos produced his first volume in Mexico City. George Parker Winship disagrees, for Stephen Daye had trained as a locksmith whereas his younger son (Matthew) had probably been apprenticed to a printer in Cambridge, England. The almanac issued by the Cambridge Press in 1647 bears Matthew's name, but that is the only surviving work to do so. Matthew Daye's successor, Samuel Green, progenitor of a long line of printers, wrote to John Winthrop the younger on July 6, 1675, that he had assumed responsibility for the press even though he had not been trained to the work. Perhaps Stephen Daye, Sr., and his older son (also named Stephen) similarly undertook at least part of the printing. Whoever printed *The Bay Psalm Book* did not have much experience. Winship observes that it "has every appearance of being an effort of beginners on a remote frontier" (Winship 1945, 30-31).

Introduction

Matthew Daye died on May 10, 1649. On July 8 of that year John Eliot wrote to Edward Winslow, "I do very much desire to translate some parts of the Scripture into [the Indian] language" (Winship 1945, 157). Six years later Eliot reported that *Genesis* had been translated and printed in Algonquin, "but our progresse is slowe, and hands short" (Winship 1945, 167). Samuel Green was complaining too; he needed more type. At the end of 1658 Eliot requested that the English Corporation for Promoting and Propogating the Gospel of Jesus Christ in New England send a printer and paper to hasten production. The Corporation responded with a new press (the second in British North America), 104 reams of paper and Marmaduke Johnson, a skilled printer.

The work then proceeded more quickly. According to Winship, "In October 1662 the Cambridge printers were producing an average of nearly ten printed pages of the INDIAN BIBLE each week" (Winship 1945, 249) and by May of the following year 1,000 copies of the first Bible printed in the English colonies appeared in Algonquin. Having completed his task, Johnson was dismissed by the Corporation and returned to England. He was back in Massachusetts in 1665 with a new press, probably financed by the colony's leading bookseller, Hezekiah Usher, who acted as agent for the Corporation. Johnson hoped to set up his new press, the colony's third, in Boston (where Usher had his store) but in 1665 and again in 1668 the General Court denied his petitions to do so. In 1674 his request was finally granted, but he died before he could enjoy the privilege given him. Still, he had taken

Introduction

an important step in the spread of printing. By 1692 Boston had replaced Cambridge as the center of publishing in New England. Indeed, by 1700 only London was producing more English books. The output of the New England presses was predominantly theological. Of the 157 items printed at Cambridge between 1638 and 1670 only 4 were poetry and 8 history or biography. Of the 133 books published in Boston between 1682 and 1698, 56 were sermons and another 39 dealt with religion. To an extent these figures reflect book-buying tastes. In 1682 Robert Boulter sent a shipment of books to John Usher, son of and successor to Hezekiah. Boulter was guessing at the taste of Bostonians based on London sales, so he included a goodly number of romances that comprised 20 percent of the stock. Usher later ordered four shipments from Boulter's successor, Richard Chiswell; among these, romances made up only 5 percent. Elizabeth Carroll Reilly's study of the accounts of the mid-eighteenth century Boston bookseller Jeremy Condy indicates that theology retained its popularity: "The libraries of colonial America, like [Condy's] account book, testify to the immense popularity of books that were religious in nature and devotional in mode" (Joyce 1983, 117-18). The divines Philip Doddridge, John Tillotson and Isaac Watts far outsold John Locke; and the most popular secular work was Alexander Pope's *Essay on Man*, which seeks "to vindicate the ways of God to man". The nature of Condy's sales reflects the character of his customers. Of the six hundred who bought on credit, a quarter were Harvard students and so likely to be des-

INTRODUCTION

tined for the ministry; another third were Harvard graduates, half of them practicing clergymen. This fondness for religious works was not, however, limited to Puritan New England. The Stiversons have examined the sales of William Hunter of Williamsburg, Virginia and found that between October 1750 and June 1752 only almanacs brought in more money than Bibles (Joyce 1983, 146). As Boynton notes, though, such figures give an incomplete picture of reading habits even in seventeenth century Massachusetts. William Brewster (d. 1644) left a library of some four hundred titles, among them Machiavelli, Richard Hakluyt and Francis Bacon. Miles Standish's collection of fifty books included Caesar's *Commentaries* and Sir Walter Raleigh's *History of the World*. Four-fifths of the thousand books belonging to the Reverend Samuel Lee (d. 1693) were in Latin.

Massachusetts sought to regulate its press, but the colony was more hospitable to printing than others such as Virginia or New York. In 1671 the governor of Virginia, Sir William Berkeley, declared: "But I thank God, there are no free schools nor printing, and I hope we shall not have these hundred years; for learning has brought disobedience, and heresy, and sects into the world, and printing has divulged them, and libels against the best government. God help us from both" (Tebbel 1972, 1). When William Nuthead attempted to set up a press in the colony in 1682, he was forced to leave. Thus Maryland received the distinction of being the second British colony to have a press (1685), and Berkeley received half his wish—printing did not come to Virginia until 1730.

Introduction

Berkeley's sentiments are echoed in the instructions James II sent to Thomas Dongan, royal governor of New York, in 1685: "And for as much as great inconvenience may arise by the liberty of printing within our province of New York, you are to provide by all necessary orders that noe person keep any press for printing, nor that any book, pamphlet or other matters whatsoever bee printed without your special leave & license first obtained" (McMurtrie 1936, 134).

The Quakers of Pennsylvania were more tolerant and it is in this state that William Bradford established a press in 1685. Like Samuel Green, Bradford begot a long line of important American printers and would himself contribute much to the book culture of the country. Bradford's first imprint, an almanac by Samuel Atkins entitled *Kalendarium Pennsylvaniense*, notes some problems facing colonial pressman of the period. In "The Printer to the Reader" Bradford observed, "Irregularities, there be in this Diary, which I desire you to pass by this year; for being lately come hither, my Materials were Misplaced, and out of order, whereupon I was forced to use Figures & Letters of various sizes" (McMurtrie 1936, 2). Atkins also commented on the limited equipment available to him: "I had thought to have incerted a Figure of the Moons Eclips, a small Draught of the form of this City, and a Table to find the hour of the day by the Shadow of a Staff; but we not having Tools to carve them in that form that I would have them . . . I pass it for this year" (Winterich 1935, 52-53). The Quakers were more concerned with the almanac's reference to "Lord Penn", the first of

INTRODUCTION

several typographical offenses that Bradford committed. The authorities appear to have been ambivalent about Bradford and his press. In 1689 he was reprimanded for printing the colony's constitution and also voted an annual salary of £40 by the Yearly Meeting. Two years later the Meeting promised to buy at least 200 copies of any book he published on the advice of the Quakers. In 1692 Bradford was jailed for printing an appeal by the dissident George Keith. Benjamin Fletcher, governor of both New York and Pennsylvania, was seeking a press to publicize his recent victory over French and Indian forces besieging Albany, so he secured Bradford's release and appointed him official printer of New York with a salary identical to that offered by the Quakers. As Massachusetts drove James Franklin to Rhode Island and Daniel Fowle to New Hampshire to become each colony's first printer, so Pennsylvania enabled New York to establish its first press in 1693.

Before the revolution printing had spread to all thirteen colonies, though Boston remained the most important center of bookselling and publishing. As late as 1773 it had more businesses engaged in the book trade (thirty) than New York and Philadelphia combined. By the end of the century that situation would change; in 1789 Boston had forty-one printers, publishers and booksellers; New York fifty-six; and Philadelphia eighty-eight. These increases reflect the growing availability of books as well as the shift in the publishing center of the country. In 1755 some 1,200 items came off the colonial presses, and these local imprints were supplemented with British im-

Introduction

ports. David Hall, Benjamin Franklin's partner, ordered more than £1000 worth of books a year from the London publisher William Strahan. Between 1760 and 1765 Jeremy Condy imported over £3500 worth of books from Joseph Richardson and lesser amounts from Thomas Longman and the firm of Kincaid and Bell of Edinburgh. In June 1752 William Hunter bought books valued at almost £300 from Samuel Birt of London and apparently issued a special catalog to advertise the collection. In 1766 John Mein of Boston was offering 1,741 titles for sale; in 1796 Robert Campbell of Philadelphia advertised 2,100 titles; and three years later H. Caritat produced a catalog of 2,700 books, a third of these fiction and adventure. These figures are far removed from the £26 worth of books that Jose Glover brought with his press in 1638.

In urban areas, then, books of all kinds were available by 1775; though they remained expensive. According to John Tebbel, "A laborer in the eighteenth century would have to work two days to buy a copy of *Roderick Random* at eight shillings, and a blacksmith would have to put in ten days' work if he wanted to buy a set of the *Spectator*, in eight volumes, at two pounds" (Tebbel 1972, 132). In the 1760s Thomas Ruddiman's *Rudiments of the Latin Tongue* cost two shillings and six pence while a pair of shoes cost less than half that at one shilling. The fifteen volume set of Tobias Smollett's *Complete History of England* sold for nine pounds, which represented three months' work for a carpenter, while a cow sold for a pound and a half. Because of their cost long novels were rarely reprinted in eighteenth century America. While the high prices reflect

INTRODUCTION

production costs, shipping was also expensive. In 1812 it cost ten cents a cubic foot to ship books from Philadelphia to New York (Tebbel 1972, 110). Outside the cities books were not only costly but also scarce. In 1857 Samuel Goodrich recalled that when he was a child in late eighteenth century rural Connecticut "the Bible and Dr. Watt's Psalms and Hymns were indispensable in every family. . . . There were, also, in the 'book shelf', a volume or two of sermons, Doddridge's 'Rise and Progress of Religion', and a very few other books and pamphlets, chiefly of a religious character" (Joyce 1983, 1). Book peddlars substituted for bookstores in such areas, and the most famous of these itinerant apostles of reading was Parson Mason Locke Weems. Although he traveled in New Jersey and New York as well as through Virginia, the Carolinas and Georgia, his primary association is with the South. While still practicing as an Episcopal clergyman he had commissioned the reprinting of sermons and other works of a religious inclination, and he then turned to authorship. In the 1790s he began his literary peregrinations "to *Englighten*, to *dulcify* and exalt human nature" (Leary 1984, 4), as he colorfully phrased his mission. Weems declared, "Humanity and Patriotism both cry aloud for Books, Books, Books" (Leary 1984, 2), so along the back roads of the South, in all kinds of weather, he followed his quest. In later years he would have his own wagon, fitted with a portable bookcase. When he was just beginning his bookselling career his accomodations were less pleasant. His letters describe his "rolling and jolting, tumbling and tossing, thru a journey

Introduction

of 200 miles, rous'd from sweet sleep at one o'clock in the morning, copp'd up in a common stage for almost three days and nights together, my head aching for loss of rest, my ears startled with female screams and masculine imprecations, [my] senses stun'd with rattling wheels, crackling whips, and clouds of dust" (Leary 1984, 22-23).

At the same time that Weems was traveling through a rural world where books often were a novelty, his employer, Matthew Carey, was contributing to the transformation of publishing. A feisty Irishman who had worked for the great French printer Didot, Carey had begun his Philadelphia career in 1785 with a $400 gift from the Marquis de Lafayette, whom Carey had met at Passy. In 1792 Carey published *Epictetus*, which Tebbel claims as the first use of Greek type in America (Tebbel 1972, 109), though Isaiah Thomas listed a font of Greek among those available to the Cambridge Press. Carey also promoted exchanges of books among printers, publishers and booksellers to increase stock inexpensively and he recognized the value of publishing a magazine to promote book sales, issuing the *Columbian Magazine* (1786) and then the *American Museum* (1787-1792). In the next century the Harpers and other publishers would adopt this practice and thereby produce important, enduring periodicals.

Another of Carey's projects was again a herald of future developments. By 1800 publishers were numerous and large enough to compete; in 1802 Carey proposed cooperation instead. The American Company of Booksellers (1802-1805) was established with Hugh Gaine, America's oldest bookseller, as president. Although the competitive

INTRODUCTION

urge soon destroyed this organization, during its brief existence it gave prizes for the best American made ink, paper and binding, thus promoting better American books. Carey's activities provide indications of development in the book industry; these changes are evident in other ways as well. In 1778 the colonial presses had produced 461 titles, and among these theology outnumbered literature 37 to 17. Twenty years later the figure had increased to 1,808. While religion accounted for 224 of these, literature was almost as plentiful (203 titles). Publishing houses were growing. From 1793 to 1796 Isaiah Thomas employed 150 people in Worcester alone, where he operated seven presses. He also owned nine others and maintained a chain of partnerships from Massachusetts to Baltimore. Altogether Thomas and his partners published some nine hundred titles, including the first American *Mother Goose* (1785), the first American novel (*The Power of Sympathy* by William Hill Brown, 1789), and perhaps the country's first edition of John Cleland's *Fanny Hill*. Even more impressive than the size of American publishing by 1800 was the quality it could now achieve. Between 1790 and 1797 Thomas Dobson of Philadelphia produced eighteen quarto volumes of the *Encyclopaedia Britannica*. It was printed on American paper and included over five hundred copperplate engravings. Barely a century earlier, in 1701, Thomas Emmes of Boston had published the first copperplate engraving in the British colonies, a portrait of Increase Mather in the minister's *Blessed Hope*. Another project reflecting the nation's progress in the book arts was William Durell's New York edition of the *Complete*

Introduction

Works of Flavius Josephus (1792-1794) in 720 folio pages, with over sixty illustrations based on the works of famous British artists. Alexander Anderson at the age of seventeen provided a number of the engravings. Anderson would become America's Thomas Bewick and help earn a respectable place for the country's illustrators. In 1810 America introduced steel engraving to the world; work in this medium and in lithography could rival European productions.

With its large publishing houses in major cities and high level of technical skill, the United States' book world of 1800 looks familiar. Yet the early nineteenth century was also what David D. Hall calls the "golden age of local publishing" (Joyce 1983, 10). Hall notes that in this period the Bible was published in twenty-four locations in Massachusetts. After 1850 only Boston and Cambridge produced them. Similarly Boston, Philadelphia and New York accounted for 50 percent of the fiction published in America between 1800 and 1810. By 1841 that figure had climbed to 92 percent (Tebbel 1972, 206).

Large and small publishers and booksellers—the two occupations became increasingly distinct—encountered a rising demand for books as literacy increased. Seventeenth century inventories indicate that about half the New Englanders owned no books. In the eighteenth century Jeremy Condy sold books to some 600 patrons in Boston, while in Williamsburg, Virginia William Parks' customers numbered perhaps 250 a year. By 1820 America produced and sold $2.5 million worth of books, and thirty years later that figure stood at $12.5 million. Tastes

INTRODUCTION

were also changing. By 1850 new and old fiction comprised the majority of titles published; and American authors, promoted by such publishers as Matthew Carey or Ticknor and Field of Boston, were at last enjoying greater popularity than their British counterparts.

Technological changes were lowering the prices of books even as demand grew. In 1813 George Clymer of Philadelphia developed an iron press that used levers rather than a screw. Three years earlier Friedrich König had invented a steam-driven press. Combined with a cylinder rather than a flat platen, such a press could print 1,100 sheets an hour. The addition of a second cylinder and other improvements allowed the press to produce four to five times that number, and by 1865 William Bullock's web press would turn out 15,000 sheets an hour. Binding also became mechanized, and improved transportation meant that the outpourings of these presses could reach the country's eager readers.

By the eve of the Civil War, a little more than two hundred years after the founding of the Cambridge Press, American publishing had expanded to include some four thousand printing offices, three thousand booksellers, and over four hundred publishers. The country was producing as many schoolbooks as all of Europe, and Harper was the world's largest publisher, with 1,549 titles in print. Harper was also the country's leading pirate of English books, introducing or popularizing the Brontes, Thackeray, George Eliot, Anthony Trollope and, later, Thomas Hardy. The thefts were not all by Americans though. In the years 1841-46 British publishers reprinted

Introduction

almost four hundred American titles, most of whose authors received no royalties, since international copyright would not exist until 1891. By 1850 American literature, like American publishing, had matured. Publishing in the United States would continue to expand, yet Boynton's decision to end his account in 1850 is sensible, for by then the book had entered the modern age.

JOSEPH ROSENBLUM

Corrections to the Original Edition

Page	For	Read
32, line 8	1842	1642
43, line 30	1786	1686
44, line 16	1785	1685
57, line 30	1793	1693
60, line 24	1789	1769
88, line 2	"The Goddards . . . Maryland." William Nuthead established Maryland's first press in St. Mary's City in 1685.	
99, line 21	1751	1754
136, line 28	Robert Aiken	Robert Aitken

SELECT BIBLIOGRAPHY

Joyce, William L., et al., eds. *Printing and Society in Early America.* Worcester, Mass.: American Antiquarian Society, 1983.

Leary, Lewis. *The Book Peddling Parson: An Account of the Life and Works of Mason Locke Weems.* Chapel Hill, N.C.: Algonquin Books, 1984.

Lehmann-Haupt, Hellmut. *The Book in America.* New York: R. R. Bowker, 1939.

Littlefield, George Emery. *Early Boston Booksellers, 1642-1711.* 1900. Reprint. New York: Burt Franklin, 1969.

McMurtrie, Douglas C. *A History of Printing in the United States.* Vol. 2, *Middle and South Atlantic States.* New York: R. R. Bowker, 1936.

Tebbel, John William. *A History of Book Publishing in the United States.* Vol. 1, *The Creation of an Industry, 1630-1865.* New York: R. R. Bowker, 1972.

Thomas, Isaiah. *History of Printing in America.* Albany, N.Y.: Joel Munsell, 1874.

Winship, George Parker. *The Cambridge Press 1638-1692.* Philadelphia: University of Pennsylvania Press, 1945.

Winterich, John T. *Early American Books and Printing.* Boston: Houghton Mifflin Co., 1935.

Wroth, Lawrence C. *An American Bookshelf, 1755.* Philadelphia: University of Pennsylvania Press, 1934.

———. *The Colonial Printer.* New York: Grolier Club, 1931. 2d enl. ed. Portland, Me.: Southworth Press, 1938.

BIOGRAPHICAL SKETCH

THE SON of George Mills and Julia (Holmes) Boynton, Henry Walcott Boynton was born in Guilford, Connecticut on April 22, 1869. He received his A.B. from Amherst in 1891 and his A.M. from the same school two years later. By this time he had become head of the Department of English Literature at Phillips Academy in Andover, Massachusetts (1892-1901). After leaving Phillips he earned his living as a professional writer. Boynton served for a time as chief reviewer for the *Atlantic Monthly*, and a number of his essays for the magazine were collected in the entertaining volume *Journalism and Literature* (1904). He also contributed to such magazines as the *Nation*, *Bookman*, *Independent*, and *Outlook*. With Thomas Wentworth Higginson he produced *A Reader's History of American Literature* (1903), and he wrote fine popular biographies of Washington Irving (1901), Bret Harte (1903), and James Fenimore Cooper (1931). Boynton also edited many texts, including Pope's *Complete Poetical Works* (1902). On the lighter side, in 1901 he published *The Golfer's Rubaiyat*, with seventy-nine quatrains like the following:

> Wake! for the sun has driven in equal flight
> The stars before him from the tee of Night,
> And holed them everyone without a Miss,
> Swinging at ease his gold-shod Shaft of Light.

Boynton was married twice. His first wife, Lucia Griswold Merrill, whom he married in 1883, died in 1899. In 1908 he married Mary Whittemore. Boynton died in Providence, Rhode Island on May 11, 1947.

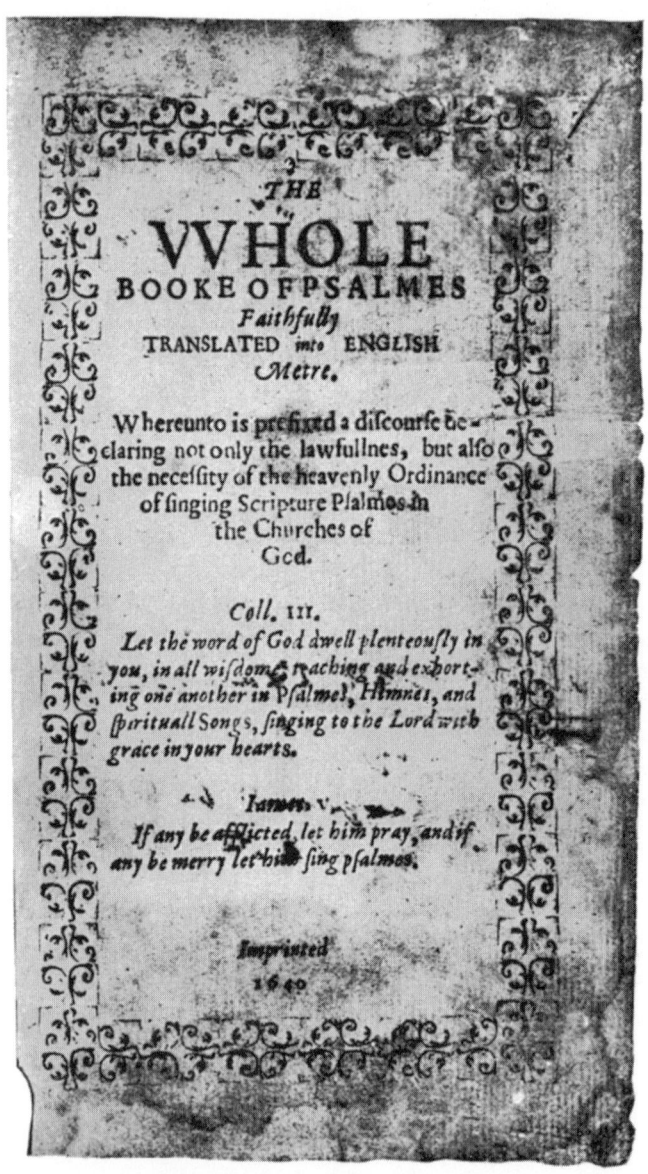

THE 'BAY PSALM BOOK': THE FIRST BOOK PRINTED IN NORTH AMERICA. FACSIMILE OF THE TITLE-PAGE OF RICHARD MATHER'S COPY, IN THE JOHN CARTER BROWN LIBRARY.

ANNALS
OF
AMERICAN BOOKSELLING
1638—1850

By
Henry Walcott Boynton

If asked Why Printers and Booksellers, I answer, they are a valuable class of the community—the friendly assistants at least if not the patrons of literature.—JOHN NICHOLS

NEW YORK
JOHN WILEY & SONS, INC.
LONDON: CHAPMAN & HALL, LIMITED
1932

COPYRIGHT, 1932
BY
HENRY WALCOTT BOYNTON

ALL RIGHTS RESERVED, INCLUDING
THE RIGHT TO REPRODUCE THIS BOOK,
OR PORTIONS THEREOF, IN ANY FORM

PRINTED IN THE UNITED STATES
OF AMERICA BY THE HADDON
CRAFTSMEN, CAMDEN, N. J.

PREFACE

THIS book essays to bring together the salient facts and persons connected with bookmaking and bookselling in the British American colonies and the young republic begotten of them. It ignores the far older achievement of the Spanish colonial culture to the south, since that culture had no direct bearing on our own, and belongs to another story. It is an informal chronicle, not a treatise. Its theme is the colonial and early nineteenth century bookseller not only as a maker of and dealer in his special commodity, but as a citizen often worth knowing in his own right. The story has engaged the chronicler largely because so many of the personæ of this old book trade were picturesque or influential figures in their time.

The narrative makes free use of dates for the sake of readers who like to keep their chronology clear. A book of annals must rightly advance from year to year, and if these pages are peppered with figures, they may easily be skipped by the date-shy.

The appended list of books may be useful to later explorers. This study hardly more than touches a field singularly rich in materials for the student of our social and intellectual past. The foot-notes refer in abbreviated form to titles given fully in the list of source books.

H. W. B.

CONTENTS

Preface	v
CHAPTER	PAGE
I. Background	1
II. Beginnings: The Cambridge Press	18
III. Bookselling in Boston, 1657-1711	34
IV. Philadelphia and New York, 1689-1723	52
V. The Franklins	65
VI. Small-Town Pioneers	83
VII. Booksellers of the Revolution: New York	98
VIII. Booksellers of the Revolution: Philadelphia and Boston	114
IX. The Post-Revolutionary Period	123
X. The Turn of the Century	138
XI. New York Arrives	152
XII. Wileys and Putnams	166
XIII. Appletons and Harpers	180
XIV. The Boston Renaissance	188
Source Books	196
Index	199

ILLUSTRATIONS

The 'Bay Psalm Book', 1640..........Frontispiece

              Page

Hubbard's 'Narrative of the Troubles with the Indians in New England', 1677.......... 29

Clough's Almanac: 'Kalendarium Nov-Anglicanum', 1705 48

Franklin imprint: 'Three Letters from the Reverend G. Whitefield', 1740............ 76

The 'Massachusetts Spy', 1774............. 119

Wall Street about 1820................... 138

Cooper's 'The Spy', 1821................. 163

The Old Corner Book Store, Boston, about 1840 188

ANNALS OF AMERICAN BOOKSELLING 1638-1850

I

BACKGROUND

WE HAVE no good word to cover all phases of production and distribution that lie between the writing function and the reading function. 'Stationer' once served in England, as *stationarius* had served in Rome. Booksellers were allied with printers, bookbinders and claspmakers, in the Stationers' Company of Shakespeare's time. The publisher as a special functionary did not exist till much later. By the early eighteenth century the word was in use, but not in our sense. Lintott was, we should say, Pope's publisher but speaks of himself as his bookseller, and mentions borrowing a horse from his own publisher, meaning the head of his production department. Another century would go by before the word approached its larger meaning. Meantime the risks of publication would continue to be taken variously by author, printer, or bookseller. If the bookseller chose to back a book, he paid the author a lump sum, or perhaps a share of the profits. If the author kept his ownership, he would sell editions of a certain number of copies, or rights of publication for a certain number of years, making his own arrangement, very likely, with the printer and binder. The method of royalty payment that has largely (not entirely) superseded these methods is an American invention less than a century old. It virtually makes the author a partner of the publisher. He stakes his time and labor on the success of his book, just as the publisher stakes his judgment and the cost of production and distribution.

In modern usage the word bookseller has shrunk as the word publisher has expanded. A good many publishers still sell books at retail, but the large majority do not. Other modern functionaries—wholesaler and jobber, and publicity man—have assumed their rôles in a highly specialized book trade. Nevertheless, for any record of the bookmaking past, 'bookselling' is still the term of richest connotation. The American bookseller, till well within a century, was commonly a printer also, or a publisher, or both. This record takes some account of him in all these aspects or offices, as well as of the kind of man he was and the part he played in his little world.

American literary historians have been naturally inclined to serve the national prestige by magnifying a purely colonial past. The history of the American colonies till the middle of the eighteenth century, at least in cultural and aesthetic matters, belongs to England as much as to modern America. Those colonists were a people far more British than Australians or

Canadians are to-day. Their aesthetic output had the customary poverty of a provincial product. They had neither time nor talent for literary effort. They had to make a place for themselves on new soil, and to wrest a living from it. They had to fight the Indians and the climate and the Devil. They must work out a practical method of government, and consolidate inch by inch the ground so painfully won from the wilderness and from tyranny across the sea. The Puritans of New England were distrustful of beauty. They had turned their backs on the literature that gave glory to the England of Elizabeth. So had the Puritans at home; Milton was their one great creative genius, and it was a miracle that Milton the poet survived Milton the zealot and controversialist. All things considered, the early colonial culture was surprisingly true to its source. Too much has been made of the provincial tendency to lag behind the mother country in matters of culture.*

Our colonial literature, for instance, was neither better nor worse than might have been expected. Its quality merits neither ridicule nor defence. For half a century the colonies had but one press, and it issued almost nothing beyond the printed matter necessary for a young community of its peculiar sort. One of our later historians, Vernon L. Parrington, has bemoaned the patriotic chroniclers' 'exaggerated regard for aesthetic values, for "the genteel tradition." . . . They have sought daintier fare than polemics, and in consequence mediocre verse has obscured political

* E.g., Wendell, 'Literary History of America.'

speculation, and poetasters have shouldered aside creative thinkers.'* Perhaps Parrington shares the weakness of the other historians in regarding our early colonial output as matter for national pride or chagrin. With some excess of ardor he enters his own special plea for the colonial makers and patrons of books. Their literature, he holds, expressed 'a world of masculine intellects and material struggles.' That is, instead of apologizing for the Wards and the Bradstreets, we should be exalting the Cottons, the Williamses, and the Mathers. The plain fact is that, throughout the seventeenth century at least, printing and bookmaking in the American colonies were of much the same character as in the English 'provinces' at home.

The first fifty years of our colonial existence coincided with a period of singular barrenness in England, so far as creative literature was concerned. The last quarter of the sixteenth century and the first quarter of the seventeenth had seen the birth, maturity, and decay of the marvelous 'Elizabethan' period, in which the genius of our race reached its highest utterance, at least in poetry and the drama. Its imaginative fecundity sprang from an impulse without parallel since the Italian Renaissance. And that impulse, as in the earlier 'rebirth,' was bound to be felt beyond the field of creative art. It too bore fruit in exploration and conquest, in religious awakening and intellectual speculation. At times the pursuit of beauty and the pursuit of truth are visibly

* Parrington, 'The Colonial Mind.'

linked, as in Bacon's 'Essays' or in the matchless prose of the King James Bible. But the sterner phase became dominant in later years. Then England forswore beauty, and dedicated herself to the service of the moral and religious idea, begotten of Calvin, that for a time would rule Britain, and for a longer time her colonies in America. We must not forget that the leaders among the first colonists of New England, as well as of Virginia, were Elizabethans born and bred. They not only survived a great creative era; they conveyed much of its vitality and ardor into the deep and narrow channel of their politico-religious obsession. Nor must we let a retroactive patriotism obscure the fact that the founders of the Massachusetts Bay Colony (if not the settlers at Plymouth) came here not as heretics but as free members of a Church of England for which they desired the restoration of ancient simplicities in rite and government. Their dissent was from method rather than doctrine. Their religious preoccupation, their distrust of aesthetic beauty and of all things 'secular' they shared with great numbers of the home-staying English of their time.

Elizabeth had not been long dead when a new spirit began to show itself among the people of England. It took the form at first of a sort of literary and intellectual fidgets. 'In the reign of the first James,' says Charles Knight, 'came an inundation of pedantry which surrounded the court with verbal criticism and solemn quibble. The people indeed had their glorious dramatists, but Bacon was looked upon as an impracticable dreamer. Controversy, too, began to be rife in England; and the spirit at last exploded in such a torrent of civil and ecclesiastical violence in the reign of James's successor, as left the many little leisure for the cultivation of their understandings. The press was absorbed by the productions of this furious spirit. There is in the British Museum a collection of 2,000 volumes of tracts issued between the years 1640 and 1660, the whole number of which several publications amounts to the enormous quantity of 30,000. . . . The number of impressions of new books unconnected with controversial subjects, during those stormy days, must have been very small. Dr. Johnson has remarked that the nation, from 1623 to 1664, was satisfied with two editions of Shakespeare's plays, which probably together did not amount to a thousand copies.'*

If these were the conditions 'at home,' what wonder that the American colonial press of the same period produced almost no pure literature? It was looked on as strictly a tool and perquisite of authority. It printed the laws, legal forms for the conduct of business, psalm books and Bibles, political and religious tracts, almanacs, and broadsides. Secular books were not forbidden, but the colonist naturally looked to the home country for such literary fare as he might crave. And here our earliest booksellers did memorable service for the struggling colonial culture. They imported much of the best (as well as some of the worst) that England produced during

* Knight, 'Shadows of the Old Booksellers.'

Background

her barren period. Later they supplied a variety of current English books for the libraries of Virginia and New England. No cultivated colonial up to the middle of the eighteenth century had to feel the lack of an aesthetic product here, with all the stores of Fleet Street and St. Paul's Churchyard to draw on. It was not till the approach of the Revolution and the dawning of a national consciousness, that American books assumed special importance in American eyes.

As for the legal restrictions laid on our early press, they were quite in line with contemporary usage in England. In its fear of 'the general diffusion of printing' the Massachusetts General Court protected the monopoly of the semi-official Cambridge press for half a century. At the end of the seventeenth century the first attempts to establish a press in Pennsylvania were at once snuffed out by authority. Until 1730 the Crown permitted no printing in Virginia. But outside of London, conditions in England were much the same during most of this period. There, too, the growth of an independent press was stoutly resisted. Even in Elizabeth's time printing had labored under many restrictions, and the curb was drawn steadily tighter by her successors.

The case of the turbulent psalmist and satirist George Wither yields some interesting evidence about the estate of the bookseller in seventeenth century London. In 1611, at the age of twenty-three, he published a book of satires and epigrams which landed him in the Marshalsea Prison. He was released by private interest, but ten years later was jailed again for similar cause. He got off this time on technical grounds, and presently won from King James a concession without precedent in England. It awarded him a monopoly for half a century of the rights of his 'Hymns and Songs of the Church,' and provided for their inclusion in all copies of the 'Psalm-Book in Meter,' which was the property of the Stationers' Company. The Company fought the claim and won, with the aid of the House of Lords. It would have been serious business if Wither had fairly established his right to ownership in his own work,—not to speak of his impudent attempt to attach it to the Company's property.

Wither was not the man to take defeat in silence, and presently issued 'The Scholler's Purgatory,' in which the grievances of authors and the faults of booksellers are fully set forth. He finds the booksellers responsible for a glut of useless publications: 'Good God! how many dungboatsfull of fruitless works do they yearly foist on his Majesty's subjects!' They threaten to dominate the Stationers' Company, an institution respectable enough in itself: 'Conceive me not, I pray you, that I go about to lay a general imputation against all stationers. For to disparage the whole profession were an act neither becoming an honest man to do, nor a prudent auditory to suffer. Their mystery (as they not untruly term it) consists of divers trades incorporated together: as printers, bookbinders, claspmakers, booksellers, etc. And of all these be some honest men, who to my knowledge are so grieved, being overborne by the notorious oppressions and proceedings of the rest, that they have wished themselves of some other calling. The printer's mystery is ingenious, painful and profitable; the bookbinder's necessary; the claspmaker's useful. And indeed, the retailer of books, commonly called a bookseller, is a trade which being well-governed and limited within certain bounds, might become somewhat serviceable to the rest. But as it is now for the most part abused, the bookseller hath not only made the printer, the binder and the claspmaker a slave to him; but hath brought authors, yea, the whole Commonwealth and all the liberal sciences into bondage. For he makes all professors of art labor for his profit, at his own price, and utters it to the Commonwealth in such fashion and at those rates which please himself.'

Here, we see, the bookseller is identified with the publisher. Elsewhere in 'The Scholler's Purgatory' Wither draws an elaborate contrast between the 'Honest Stationer,' who has all the virtues, and the 'Mere Stationer' who has all the vices, of his order. The Mere Stationer 'imagines he was born altogether for himself, and exerciseth his Mystery without any respect to the glory of God or the public advantage. . . . may well be termed the Devil's seedsman, seeing he is the aptest instrument to sow schisms, heresies, scandals, and seditions through the world. . . .

He praises no book but what sells well, and that must be his own copy too, or else he will have some flirt at it. . . . He makes no conscience what trash he puts off; nor how much he takes for that which is worth nothing. He will not stick to belie his author's intentions, or to publish secretly that there is somewhat in his new imprinted books against the State or some honorable personages; that so, they being questioned, his ware may have the quicker sale. . . . If he get any written copy into his power likely to be vendible, whether the author be willing or no he will publish it. . . . Nay, he often gives books such names as will in his opinion make them saleable, when there is little or nothing in the whole volume suitable to such a title.'

Bless us! we rub our eyes and wonder if all this can really have been written three centuries ago! The Honest Stationer, please note, gets full credit at George Wither's hands, even in the dubious phase of bookseller. At his best, he is no 'Mere Bookseller, that is, one who selleth merely ink and paper bundled up together for his own advantage only, but he is a Chapman of the Arts. . . . The reputation of scholars is as dear to him as his own; for he acknowledgeth that from them his mystery hath both beginning and means of continuance. He loves a good author as his brother, and will be ready to yield him the due portion of his labors without wrangling.' A noble fellow, that bookseller-publisher, molded to the heart's desire of authors in any age. For in the bookish arts, as in other human affairs, there is little new under the sun.

On the whole it is likely that the trials of the author have had a fuller airing than the very considerable difficulties and complications of the bookseller and the publisher, who in the nature of things are less vocal and articulate. In George Wither's time the way of the bookseller was particularly hard. Under Elizabeth every book offered for printing was supposed to be censored and licensed by the Queen or by certain members of her Privy Council. This office of supervision, to be sure, was soon left to the Stationers' Company. The business of manufacturing and selling books, in those days, was held in no esteem by persons of quality. A stationer or bookseller of sixteenth century England was nearly as shabby a fellow, socially considered, as a playwright or even an actor. No polite author would descend to deal with the book trade. Sir Philip Sidney permitted none of his work to be set in vulgar type. The 'Arcadia' might decently be circulated in manuscript among friends of his own order, that was all. Professional scriveners still made a living at copying such work. If some scurvy stationer of St. Paul's Churchyard got hold of a copy and mauled it into print, it was no matter of interest among gentlemen. Even a common player like William Shakespeare could show supreme indifference to the printed form of his work. The world owes much to the unscrupulous scavengers who rescued so many Elizabethan treasures from the theatrical rubbish-heap. There was the malodorous and piratical Danter, a professional trafficker in scurrilous and 'curious' stuff (his offspring are still active in the purlieus of the book world). It was he who printed 'Titus Andronicus' (which might have been spared), and 'Romeo and Juliet,' which was, we now see, a stone in the foundation: for what would our theatre or literature have been without 'Romeo' in the background? Shakespeare had no hand in the publishing of these plays, or of any of the fourteen others that were printed in his lifetime. Most of them were sadly bungled and mangled in the process. The author simply didn't care, or he could have done something to protect his offspring. He was a member of the Lord Chamberlain's Company, and that powerful person could easily, through his control of the Stationers' Company, have restrained the grosser forms of piracy. As for a copyright law, there was none to protect an author, nobody seems to have thought such protection in order. Among the stationers there was a rule of first come first served. The original sponsor of a book in English established his rights in it by entering the title of the book, depositing a copy with the Stationers' Company, and paying a fee of sixpence. The title was then his personal property. Any profit for the author was a matter of indulgence or policy. A writer might (if he were sordid enough) extract a cash payment from the prospective publisher and proprietor of a new work, on turning over the manuscript. It is easy to understand what a pother there was among the members of the Stationers' Company when George Wither was impudent enough to establish ownership in his own book, by a privately obtained concession from the Crown.

The stationers had plenty of troubles to face as the years went on. The doings of the Star Chamber against independent or seditious printers (which meant much the same thing) are familiar history. When the Puritan Prynne wrote his attack on the British stage, 'Histrio-Mastix,' he was fined $5,000, disbarred, pilloried, had his ears cropped, and was sentenced to prison for life; his printer Starke was also fined and pilloried. Three years later, a year before the Cambridge press was set up in our Bay Colony, the Star Chamber clamped the lid on printting and publishing in England. Only a score of printers were to be licensed in all Britain. All books were to be strictly censored, to be entered in the Stationers' Register, and to bear the names of printer and author. One of the regulations then imposed (as Mumby suggested twenty years ago) 'would be most thankfully received by most members of the book trade of to-day: "that no haberdasher of small wares, ironmonger, chandler, or shopkeeper," or any other person not regularly apprenticed in the trade, should "receive, take or buy to barter or sell again, change or do away" any books whatsoever, without severe penalties.'* However, all these rulings became a dead letter when, in 1641, the Long Parliament put an end to the Star Chamber. Then followed a general dis-

* Mumby, 'Romance of Bookselling.'

regard of legal restrictions on printing. But meanwhile the whole atmosphere and bias of the time had grown indifferent if not hostile to the writing and publishing of purely imaginative work. Instead of the mighty galaxy of Elizabethans were only Milton and Dryden and Bunyan, Walton and Waller, and the race of procurers who produced the literary and dramatic salacities that satisfied Charles and his court.

But if seventeenth century England, under Puritan and Cavalier alike, was relatively barren of great literature, it laid the foundations of modern science and technology. It laid the foundation, for instance, of both the rationalism and the scientific ardor of the modern world. In its first years Bacon dared to ignore theology and to exalt 'natural philosophy, the great mother of the sciences.' Even before the end of the Civil War, London had a group of men who found escape from political and religious hysteria in the laboratory of science. In 1648 an Oxford Society was formed whose business was 'to discourse and consider of philosophical enquiries and such as related thereto, as Physick, Anatomy, Geometry, Astronomy, Navigation, Statics, Magnetics, Chymicks, Mechanicks, and Natural Experiments: with the state of these studies, as then cultivated at home and abroad.'

When the Restoration came, many of these men helped found a greater scientific nucleus in London. Charles himself named it the Royal Society in token of his interest in scientific research and experiment. The laboratory became a playground for courtiers like Buckingham. Charles himself took the trouble to learn something of subjects like chemistry and navigation. Poets like Denham and Cowley gained prestige by membership in the Society. 'Its definite establishment marks the opening of a great age of scientific discovery in England. Almost every year of the half-century that followed saw some step made to a wider and truer knowledge. Our first national observatory rose at Greenwich, and modern astronomy began with the long series of astronomical observations which immortalized the name of Flamsteed. His successor, Halley, undertook the investigation of the tides, of the comets, and of terrestrial magnetism. Hooke improved the microscope, and gave a fresh impulse to microscopical research. Boyle made the air-pump a means of advancing the science of pneumatics, and became the founder of our experimental chemistry. Wilkins pointed forward to the science of philology in his scheme of a universal language. Sydenham introduced a careful observation of nature and facts, which changed the whole face of medicine. The physiological researches of Willis first threw light upon the structure of the brain. Woodward was the founder of mineralogy. In his edition of Willoughby's "Ornithology," and in his own "History of the Fishes," John Ray was the first to raise zoology to the rank of a science, and the first scientific classification of animals was attempted in his "Synopsis of Quadrupeds." Modern botany began with his "History of Plants," and the researches of an Oxford professor, Robert Morrison; while Grow divided with Malpighi the credit of founding the study of vegetable physiology.'*

And these names were all dwarfed by the name of Newton, whose new theory of the universe revolutionized and directed the course of science till our own time. So began a long battle between tradition and faith on the one side and reason and experiment on the other. Books, except as a medium for light diversion, became the vehicles of dispute or instruction. Following Parrington's hint, turning our backs on mere literary considerations, we see better what the seventeenth century really achieved. It produced, at least, a great number of schoolbooks, texts, dictionaries, works on geography, and treatises on the new science. And many of these, deeply as the scientific spirit was distrusted by Puritanism, found their way to the American colonies and profoundly influenced our eighteenth century culture and morale.

This much background we need as a basis for the annals that follow. The story of England in the seventeenth century is our own story from beginning to end. Shakespeare did not die till 1616, two years after the Dutch fur-traders gained foothold at Albany; nine years after John Smith landed at Jamestown. The First Folio of the Plays did not appear till 1623,

* J. R. Green, 'Short History of the English People.'

three years after certain broad-collared individualists blundered across the Atlantic and rang up the curtain on a new tragicomedy of human affairs at sandy Plymouth and along the hilly foreshores of Massachusetts Bay.

II

BEGINNINGS

A SINGULAR mark of the Massachusetts Bay settlers was their early preoccupation with book learning. The Pilgrims at Plymouth were the physical pioneers of the North, broke ground there for the white man's 'civilization,' but they were simple folk, mainly farmers. Elder Brewster was the only university man aboard the *Mayflower:* he had been at Cambridge for a year or so. And the men of Plymouth were separatists, had deliberately cut loose from a Church of England tradition in which learning, scholarship, was a primary ingredient. The settlers of the Massachusetts Bay Company, on the other hand, were dissenters, nonconformists. They wished to change or restore the old religion, not to abandon it. And when before long they did throw over the rule and rites of the English Church for the simpler 'Congregational way,' they had no thought of abandoning the culture in which they had been reared. Their leaders included many of the notable scholars of the time, Puritan zealots, yet steeped in pagan letters and vowed to scholarship. These men ruled the colony as both ministers and magistrates. The 'meeting house' was a place for worship and also for practical affairs.

Lawyers were banned from the colony; politics were reduced to a 'Thus saith the Lord.' Neither social equality nor political democracy was dreamed of; religious tolerance meant lack of faith. And for this Puritan theocracy, as for every absolutism whether of Czar, Pope, or Soviet, the only safety lay in an absolute maintenance of the *status quo*.

This powerful clergy, therefore, must continue to rule by virtue of its scholarship as well as its piety. Its prestige, like that of mandarin or medicine-man, hung upon the mystery of Learning. A bare six years after John Winthrop became first Governor of the Massachusetts Bay Colony, a step was taken toward assuring the succession of learned divines who should lead the colonists on the strait and narrow path. In 1636 the General Court appropriated £400 for the establishment of a 'school or college' at Newtown, 'to advance learning and perpetuate it to posterity; dreading to leave an illiterate ministry to the churches when our present ministers shall lie in the dust.' Two years later a young minister, John Harvard, died a bachelor and bequeathed to the infant academy or college his name, half his estate (about £780), and a library of some three hundred books. Newtown thereupon became 'Cambridge' in honor of the English nursery where John Harvard and at least fourscore of the early Massachusetts leaders were reared. To this new seed-bed of learning was brought, almost at once, the first printing press used in North

America, and the first collection of books offered there for sale.

The founder or begetter of colonial printing and bookselling was a nonconformist clergyman of the Church of England, Jesse Glover. He was one of a group of pious and well-to-do dissenters who, after the Massachusetts Bay Company yielded its authority to the Massachusetts Bay Colony, continued to work actively for the welfare of their brethren in America. Already the colonial theocracy wished to have the means of publishing its will. Laws must be printed, sermons, proclamations, and psalm books. Glover contributed, and collected from friends 'in England and Holland,' enough money to buy a press and types. He himself would take charge of the enterprise and cast his lot, for awhile at least, with the elect of New England. In the summer of 1638 he embarked in the *John of London* with a wife, five children, a press, a printer; and a goodly number of books to be disposed of among the colonists. The press would be set up in the shadow of the new college, under authority of the General Court. Everything was neatly arranged. The only slip in the proceedings was the death of Glover during the voyage: a loss, but not a fatal loss, for his widow at once took over his affairs as a matter of course, thereby establishing precedent for a long line of colonial relicts whose achievements in printing and bookselling will be touched on in this chronicle. The old-fashioned woman did no advertising, but when her man died she carried on. It was so in colonial times, it has always been so more than we realize, though while it was the fashion for women to seem helpless and dependent, the world contrived to ignore all evidence to the contrary.

The widow Glover, we must own, makes no powerful showing in the story. Reporting at Cambridge with her brood of children, her press and types, and her printer Stephen Daye, she placed them all in the receptive hands of the president of the new college, the Rev. Henry Dunster. The legal status of the press in relation to the college seems to have been undefined for some time. According to Harvard records, Glover actually 'gave to the college a font of printing letters, and some gentlemen of Amsterdam gave towards furnishing of a printing press.' But it does not appear that the press belonged at any time to the college. It was the property of the widow Glover, and President Dunster presently married them both and took them into his house. Years later, after her death, the press was legally declared the property of her son John. Dunster had to make restitution of sundry other articles also, as well as a sum of money; against which, in a counterclaim, he was careful to enter all possible charges for the rearing and education of said John. He was a pious man, and seems to have done his duty by his stepchildren among a multitude of duties that fell to him as head of the college. He served not only as president but as treasurer and chief steward; all details of management and discipline were in his hands. There was little money to work with. The students' fees and bills were generally paid in sheep, wheat, butter, malt, and cotton. Often the president had trouble collecting his small salary, and more than once it was cut. If the inconsiderable profits of his wife's printing press went straight into the domestic hopper, they can have only helped toward feeding and clothing her five children. And he was soon busy producing by a second marriage five children of his own. Still, it must be owned that other actions of recovery against the Rev. Mr. Dunster, by other complainants, are in the record. He was a colonial Englishman, the true Yankee was a bird of later hatching; but the religiosity of those earliest Puritans was not always linked to fastidiousness in practical affairs. As a peppery Boston bookseller of a century later remarked, by way of animating certain delinquent customers, ' 'Tis great pity a Soil that will bear Piety so well, should not produce a tolerable Crop of Common Honesty.'

President Henry Dunster was by no means an ordinary man. He came to New England for his soul's sake, a distinguished scholar and orientalist whom the General Court at once drafted for difficult public service. He served well. As we have seen, Harvard College, like Oxford and Cambridge in England, and the later New England colleges, was founded not to educate the general, but as a school of divinity. Fifty years after its founding, Cotton Mather, in bilious mood, complained that Harvard offered but narrow privileges to its 'forty or fifty children, few of them capable of edification by those exercises.' But the records show stiff requirements for admission from the beginning, and a curriculum much like that of Oxford or Cambridge at the time. Many of the early Harvard graduates achieved high preferment in Church and State, in the old England as well as the New. One zealous apologist for Puritan scholarship says, 'Under Dunster and Chauncy the standards were undoubtedly as high here as in England. That this was recognized in England is evident from the fact that a number of boys of good family were sent over here to Harvard to be educated.'* For such a race as these colonials, for such a dynasty certainly as these men who led them, good schooling was a necessary of life: so were books, and the means of printing books. No sooner the college than the press. At Cambridge, in the president's own house, Stephen Daye set up the Glover printing equipment; and there it stayed and functioned till after Dunster's retirement. This first colonial printer was not an expert at his task. Daye was a locksmith by trade who knew something about presswork but little about composition. A triviality of fame connects his name rather than Glover's or Dunster's with the first American books. None of the books he produced bears his name. Fate decreed that he should print, rather badly, the first few books issued in the American colonies: a book of laws, some college lists, catechisms, sermons, almanacs, and above all, the famous 'Bay Psalm Book,' the work of some of the colony's most eminent divines. Stephen Daye did as well as he could

* Wright, 'Literary Culture of Early New England.'

for a few years, which was not very well, was retired in favor of his son Matthew about 1646, and lived on in Cambridge at his old trade of locksmith.

Another cause for remembering Glover and Dunster is the existence and fate of the considerable store of books brought over on the *John of London*, not as a private library but for sale. Dunster took over from Glover the rôle of bookseller as well as of husband and head-printer. Our American book trade therefore started fairly abreast of its normal handmaidens, authorship and typography. How many Glover books there were and how many the august bookseller disposed of, we know not. Littlefield says: 'Mr. Dunster sold the books . . . but in right of his wife and as president of the College he retained the press, which he managed and from which he received the profits.'* In the list of charges allowed by the court against Dunster in 1656 in favor of Glover's son John, is an item 'for sale of Bookes,' of £26 10/. And Dunster's side of the ledger is credited with the return to John Glover of 'all Mr. Glover's Books unsold, to be delivered according to Cattalogue.' Clearly Dunster held the books on the same terms as the press, as his wife's property, and carried out Glover's intention by selling them as he could. Twenty-six pounds, according to inventories of the period, would have represented from two hundred to three hundred books. Dunster probably bought in some of them for the college library, in which he was keenly interested.

* Littlefield, 'Early Boston Booksellers.'

BEGINNINGS 25

Others he would have sold to the gentleman-parsons of the colony, who, we know, were eager for books from the beginning. This was true of the settlers as a whole, even in Plymouth where the standard of literacy was so much lower than in the neighbor colony. Governor Bradford owned that 'prior to 1650 Harvard College neither received from Plymouth nor contributed to that place more than one or two persons.'* Yet various inventories of ordinary estates in early Plymouth show that the family books were commonly valued at a tenth to a fifth of the total property. At his death in 1644 Elder Brewster left a library of some four hundred titles, many of which were published after 1620 and must have been bought soon after their issue in England. The list shows the usual preponderance of theological and political writing, but also Bacon's 'Advancement of Learning,' Machiavelli, Hakluyt, Wither, and Dekker. Bluff Miles Standish left fifty books, including Caesar's 'Commentaries' and Raleigh's 'History of the World.' If new books were reaching these first men of Plymouth, they were far more readily available for the scholars of Massachusetts Bay. Consignments from England were being sent to both Winthrops as early as 1631, as well as catalogues of the German 'book fairs,' from which they ordered liberally. The colonists of New England, says Wright, 'during the first half century of their existence were able, as far as they desired, to keep in touch with political, scientific and literary

* Bradford, 'History of Plymouth.'

men and activities in England, and, beyond any of England's colonies at any time in her history, during the period of colonization, they felt a desire for these things.'* In short, these colonists, whose isolation has been so often stressed, were by no means cut off from the home country. They made little of the hard voyage there and back, whether for business or pleasure. There was constant interchange of persons and ideas between the old England and the New. On the establishment of the Commonwealth a score and more of the Massachusetts Bay ministers chose to return to a mother-country where they could once more be useful and at peace. At the Restoration, fourteen ministers came (or came back) here to escape persecution. Says Wright: 'It is interesting to speculate upon the possibility that, had he been accorded harsher treatment, Milton might himself have followed the Regicides to America, in which case "Paradise Lost" would have been written in New England—or not at all.'† Milton was on friendly terms with a number of his fellow-countrymen and fellow-nonconformists who chanced to be on this side of the water, especially with Roger Williams and the younger Winthrop. Winthrop was made a fellow of the Royal Society within two years of the Society's founding, and other colonists were recognized by it from the beginning. The elder Winthrop was a correspondent of many of the greatest men of England and the continent, including Sir Thomas Browne, Camden,

---

* Wright, 'Literary Culture of Early New England.'
† *Ibid.*

Cromwell, Charles II, Milton, Newton, Galileo, Herbert of Cherbury, Prince Rupert, Sir Henry Wotton, and Christopher Wren. All this goes to show that among the rulers of the Massachusetts Bay Colony, and even among the rank and file of the settlers, there was a demand for books hardly to be touched by our single press. A few years after that press was founded, the Boston neighborhood would have its own bookseller to handle the Cambridge product, such as it was, and also to import books from 'home.'

But before we begin our proper chronicle of colonial bookselling, something must be said of the famous Cambridge Press and its product. Its first real book, 'The Whole Booke of Psalmes,' generally called 'The Bay Psalm Book,' is the only book printed by Stephen Daye that has life in it except for bibliographers and students of colonial history. Sternhold and Hopkins in England had produced a psalm book in English for congregational use. It bore the same title, and was a version rude enough but not without poetic quality. The divines of the Massachusetts Colony wanted something altogether untainted by imagination or beauty of form. Within half a dozen years after the colony was founded they had collaborated upon a psaltery sufficiently hand-hewn for their grim taste. Richard Mather, founder of the Mather tribe, and good John Eliot were among the authors. Mather wrote the famous preface: 'If the verses are not always so smooth and elegant as some desire and expect, let them consider that God's altar needs not pollishings; we have respected rather a plaine translation than to smooth our verses with the sweetness of any paraphrase, and soe have attended conscience rather than elegance, fidelity rather than poetry. . . .'

The 'Bay Psalm Book' has been much laughed at, but its quaintness does not belong to its New England provincialism. The book did not seem comic or crude to nonconformists in England, nor did other sixteenth century American colonial books. Wigglesworth's 'Day of Doom,' grotesque as it is to modern ears, was twice reprinted in England. The 'Bay Psalm Book' went through eighteen editions in England and twenty-two in Scotland, the last in 1759. It was still popular in England after the version of Tate and Brady had supplanted it in America. And in general the publications of the Cambridge press were not out of line with those of the dissenting press abroad. Its almanacs, sermons, political tracts, were paralleled in the lists of contemporary printing in England. Wright is justified in saying that 'If no great literature was produced by the Puritans in New England, it may be not because they were in New England, but because little great literature was produced by the Puritans anywhere.'* In short, the colonial output may fairly be compared not with the best that contemporary England could produce, but with the product of other provincial regions. Outside London, seventeenth century publication was almost negligi-

* Wright, 'Literary Culture.'

A NARRATIVE

OF THE TROUBLES WITH THE

INDIANS

In *NEW-ENGLAND*, from the first planting thereof in the year 1607. to this present year 1677. But chiefly of the late Troubles in the two last years, 1675. and 1676.

To which is added a Discourse about the *Warre* with the

PEQUODS

In the year 1637.

By W. Hubbard, *Minister of* Ipswich.

And the Lord said unto Moses, write this for a Memoriall in a Book, and rehearse it in the ears of Joshua; for I will utterly put out the Remembrance of Amalek from under heaven. Exod. 17. 14.

Wherefore it is said in the book of the warrs of the Lord, what he did in the red sea, and in Brooks of Arnon. Numb. 21. 14.

As cold waters to a thirsty soul, so is good news from a far Country. Prov. 25. 25.

Expressa Imago, et quasi speculum quoddam viæ humanæ est historia, quia talia vel similia semper possunt in mundo accidere. *Thucyd.*

Historia tradit quæ facta sint, et quæ semper sint futura, donec eadem manet hominum natura. *Idem.*

Historiæ cognitio rutissima institutio, et præparatio est ad actiones politicas, et illustris Magistra ad perferendas fortunæ vices. *Pol. b.*

Published by Authority.

BOSTON;
Printed by *John Foster*, in the year 1677.

HUBBARD'S 'NARRATIVE': JOHN FOSTER WAS THE FIRST BOSTON PRINTER AND THE FIRST COLONIAL ENGRAVER. THIS BOOK CONTAINS THE FIRST AMERICAN-MADE MAP OF NEW ENGLAND.

ble. The first press in Glasgow was set up only a year earlier than the Cambridge press. Manchester had no printing till 1732, and Liverpool till 1751. Finally, the average quality of books printed here in the seventeenth century was lowered by the colonists' habit of publishing their more pretentious efforts in England. They wished their work to have a chance with the home audience. So it came about that even controversial writing was printed in London, and disputes between next-door neighbors like Roger Williams and John Cotton went on by way of the high seas and St. Paul's Churchyard. Williams's 'Bloody Tenent' was issued in London in 1644, John Cotton's reply in 1647, and Williams's rejoinder in 1652!

Samuel Green, the Dayes' successor at Cambridge, had, like Stephen Daye, little training for his task, being (unlike Daye) a better compositor than printer. He improved with practice, and was founder of a dynasty of printers and booksellers who shone in both crafts, for nearly two centuries, all the way from Massachusetts to Virginia. But Samuel Green was not an expert; and when the time came to print John Eliot's Bible for the Indians, the London Society for the Propagation of the Gospel sent over a skilled printer named Marmaduke Johnson. A recent historian, James Truslow Adams, says some strange things about the attitude of the first colonists toward the Indians. He says they had 'no interest in the Indian as a human being—cared nothing for saving his soul. . . . There was some talk now and then of the glory of converting the heathen, but for the most part little or nothing was ever done toward that end. The Reverend John Eliot . . . was almost the only person who ventured to think of the Indian as a soul to be saved rather than a child of the devil to be fought when need be.'*

In fact, all the records show that the early New England settler took his Indians quite seriously as human beings to be lived with and souls to be saved. His conduct toward the savage was dubious from the first; but his attitude was admirable. The eight or ten thousand red men of New England could not be ignored by a population of white interlopers who were still a minority when Harvard was founded. Provision was made for Indian students at the college, and the second charter of the college (1650) declared its object to be 'the education of the English and Indian youth of this country in knowledge and godliness.' Ten years later a brick building, 'the Indian College,' stood in the college yard. Further, a glance at a list of the early publications of the Cambridge press discovers a number dedicated to the education and conversion of the red man. The Society for the Propagation of the Gospel and the saintly John Eliot were not looked on as fanatics. Time, not current opinion, decided that they were wasting their effort, and that the only good Indian (from the practical point of view) was the dead one. Once enlightened on that head, the colonists could go forward boldly in the necessary work of wiping out a breed

* Adams, 'Epic of America.'

of 'devilish men who serve nothing but the Devil.' Yet as late as 1715, William Bradford in New York was issuing a Mohawk prayer book. Certainly in the beginning there was a real impulse to conquer the heathen for Christ by gentler means than extermination or even banishment. So John Eliot solemnly worried the scriptures into the Algonquin tongue, and Marmaduke Johnson of London was sent over to put that gibberish for the first time into type.

Alas, the Devil was not altogether idle even among the elect. There were strange frailties known in the grim settlements at Plymouth and along the Bay. The printer Marmaduke Johnson had been chosen for his skill with the type-case rather than for his moral virtue. He left a wife in London, and presently came near being sent back to her, for toying with the affections of a young daughter of his master Samuel Green of Cambridge. But he seems to have been too useful to be dispensed with, the affair was smoothed over. After working with Green for some years, Johnson set up a press of his own in Cambridge, and in 1674 got permission from the General Court of the colony to move his establishment to Boston. No printing, up to that time, had been permitted anywhere outside of Cambridge. There was too much danger for the theocracy in an unlicensed production and diffusion of secular print. As we have seen, England had a similar fear of the press at that time. Printing was not permitted in English provincial towns till 1673. It was forbidden by the Crown in Virginia till 1730, a century after the 'Bay Psalm

Book' was printed in Massachusetts.* So Johnson's winning of a license to set up a press in Boston was a notable event. Unluckily, just as he had gained the privilege he died.

But printerless Boston had possessed a bookseller for a full generation. Hezekiah Usher was living in Cambridge when Harvard College and the Cambridge press were founded. In 1842 he moved to Boston, bought property there, and prospered as a general merchant. He exported or imported furs, fish, beef, grain, lumber, sugar, oil, wine, cotton; and books. The first absolute record of his bookselling belongs to the year 1647. In course of time, books became an important part of his business. He was agent of the English Society for the Propagation of the Gospel. He marketed the product of the press across the Charles. Various issues of the Cambridge press were 'printed for' Hezekiah Usher or his son John; which would seem to mean that the Ushers took the risks of (or 'published') such issues. Hezekiah Usher became a rich man and a prominent citizen, was State Representative for several terms, a founder of the Old South Church, and an officer of the Artillery Company—sure sign of social acceptance. He lived long enough to be in peril of the witch-hanging madness, was actually charged with witchcraft in the dolorous year 1692: 'But on account of the goodness of his character he was, by con-

* Wroth, 'Colonial Printer.'

nivance, allowed to secrete himself in the house of a friend and afterward to escape out of the hands of his persecutors, until the delusion or madness of the time subsided, and reason restored the balm of tranquillity to the public mind.'*

* Thomas, 'History of Printing.'

III

BOOKSELLING IN BOSTON, 1657-1711

Much had happened to the Bay Colony's character and culture during that first half-century. Time had wiped out the generation of British-born scholars who founded Boston and Cambridge. Local interests and local gossip held the foreground, for a people who had little leisure or license for diversion. There was small social contact with the other colonies. The population grew fast, yet living conditions improved but slowly. Roads hardly existed; carriages were not used. The Indian menace was continual and increasing, till the death of Philip established once for all the dominion of the white men. Meanwhile authority began to be challenged. The country people in particular grew impatient of the church-and-state tyranny fostered by the Mathers and their crew. There was little book learning for these people; a few passable schools in and near Boston, none in New York or in the back country. But in New England, as in the colonies to the south, 'the people were to a great extent opposed to the expenditure of public money for school purposes and the old picture of every village with its free school and a population athirst for learning is a pure figment of the imagination. Such schools as were

operated under the laws and were called free, required the payment of tuition from all but those pupils whose parents were too poor to afford it, and were consequently quite different from our modern public schools. There was nothing democratic about them and it was not intended that there should be.'*
William Penn had proposed to establish public schools in his domain, but it was not done. New York was indifferent. New England laws for the maintenance of schools in all communities of a certain number of inhabitants were ignored. Illiteracy increased. In 1698 in the town of Natick, near Boston, only one child in seventy could read. Twenty years later eight out of the thirteen proprietors of Manchester in New Hampshire could not write their names.

Yet it is clear that at this time there was a considerable market for books, at least in the immediate neighborhood of Boston. Private collections were growing. Books were imported by the puncheon, butt, or hogshead. One hogshead as invoiced contained books worth £57 6/. The Harvard library grew steadily. In 1657 Boston built its Town House partly to house a public library, the first in the colonies. 'As in London the booksellers clustered around St. Paul's and the exchange, so in Boston they gathered around the Town House.'† Chiswell, the famous London book dealer, had large dealings with John Usher and other Boston booksellers. Boulter

* Adams, 'Provincial Society.'
† Ford, 'Boston Book Market.'

was another London exporter of some account. One consignment of 125 titles he sent to John Usher on speculation shows that there must have been a market in Boston for items difficult to square with Puritan theory. The list includes many romances in duplicate, Sidney's 'Arcadia,' collections of poetry, jest-books, and even playing cards. Increase Mather's library was by no means confined to pious works. It contained a representative assembly of the Latin and Greek classics, and works by Milton, Bacon, Herbert. And among the books available for young Cotton Mather in the family library were Aesop, Plautus, and—Ovid's 'Art of Love'! For all the learned class, which is to say the churchly class, though theological and controversial books predominated, the pagan classics were part of their heritage. The library of the Rev. Samuel Lee of Bristol (who died in 1693), with its thousand titles, was made up almost altogether of foreign books, four-fifths of them in Latin. Some of these volumes no doubt had passed through the hands of Boston booksellers. It is true that this classical treasure, so cherished by the leaders of the Bay Colony, was looked on uneasily by some of the faithful. Even Governor Winthrop, with his relatively liberal tastes, seems to have had qualms, and we find a friend, Thomas Shepard, reassuring him: 'Your sudden apprehensions against reading and learning heathen authors I persuade myself were suddenly suggested, and will easily be answered by B. Dunstar, if you should impart them to him.' We can but wonder what Bro. Dunster, as a

Puritan, found to say in defence of the Ovids, Horaces, and Juvenals that were to be found on the shelves of the New England divines. Strange creatures have found shelter under the academic gown, since scholarship began; antiquity carries its own special immunities.

The product of the Cambridge press was watched narrowly enough. Official censorship was always in the offing, though seldom invoked. Marmaduke Johnson and Bartholomew Green were fined on occasion for reprinting without permission 'The Isle of Pines'; a narrative 'of the Baron Munchausen order'; and an English version of Thomas à Kempis's 'Imitatio Christi' was suppressed, while printing, as the utterance of 'a Popish minister, wherein is contained some things that are less safe to be diffused among the people of this place.' Importations were less easily regulated. They included not only 'the classics,' but much contemporary pamphleteering from England, as well as schoolbooks and publications of the new Royal society, sound treatises on law, and fantastic manuals of medicine. As in England, though more slowly, a taste for secular literature was growing as the century ran out. And the English booksellers who came over with their wares, or dealt at arm's length with the colonial trade, would naturally offer what was most popular at home, and dispose of some of it. No doubt there was literary bootlegging among the rasher spirits of old Boston. Activity there certainly was, toward the end of the century. Within fifty years after Hezekiah Usher began selling books, the names of a dozen Boston dealers were appearing on the imprints of pamphlets and almanacs, and upon invoices of books from abroad.

Many of these men were printers at one time or another. Marmaduke Johnson, we recall, had been unlucky enough to die just after getting his license to set up the first press in Boston. The concession did not lapse, but was taken over together with Johnson's printing equipment by a promising young colonial who actually became the first printer in the colonies outside Cambridge. He was at work at his press in 1675, and selling books a year later. He was a notable person in his time, about whom a good book has been written,* and whom an admirer has pronounced 'one of the great men of that age,—a scholar, printer, engraver, chemist,—a man worthy of the love, friendship and admiration of the Mathers. Had Foster lived to the age that Franklin reached, Franklin might have been called "a second Foster."' If this is pressing the point, Foster really deserves being kept in memory among the men of his time and place. He was a Harvard man, and came third in the list of his class. These lists were arranged, then and for a century after, not alphabetically or by scholarship, but by social rank. Foster's father was a member of the General Court and a captain of militia. There was little ahead for a college man who did not enter the ministry. Printing and bookselling were at least a door out of that fold. Thomas says John Fos-

* Green, 'John Foster.'

ter probably knew little or nothing of printing when he began, 'but having obtained permission to print he employed workmen, carried on printing in his own name, and was accountable to government for the productions of his press. . . . If Foster's printing equalled, it could not be said to excel that of Green or Johnson, either in neatness or correctness.'*

But he was more than a printer if less than a fine printer. He was the first American engraver, illustrated a number of books of his own printing, and left behind a print of his friend Increase Mather that shows real talent for portraiture. He was a considerable bookseller and publisher. He supplied the astronomical calculations for his almanacs, and had much reputation for scientific acquirement. When he died at the age of thirty-three, he was greatly mourned, and a number of poetical tributes were offered to his memory as bookseller and astronomer. Some lines by a Massachusetts parson include a passage quoted by Isaiah Thomas with a demure comment which seems justified by the evidence:

> Thy body, which no activeness did lack,
> Now's laid aside like an old Almanack;
> But for the present only's out of date,
> 'T will have at length a far more active state.
> Yea, though with dust thy body soiled be,
> Yet at the resurrection we shall see
> A fair EDITION and of matchless worth,
> Free from ERRATAS, new in Heaven set forth;

* Thomas, 'History of Printing.'

'T is but a word from God the great Creator,
It shall be done when he saith *Imprimatur*.

Thomas's comment is, 'Whoever has read the celebrated epitaph by Franklin, on himself, will have some suspicion that it was taken from this *original*.' Isaiah Thomas, as we shall see, had a less flattering opinion of Franklin's probity than was or is commonly held. Another commentator, however, has discovered that the figure goes back, perhaps to some more distant original, certainly as far as Benjamin Woodbridge's elegy on John Cotton, who died in 1652, which closes:

> O what a monument of glorious worth
> When in a new edition he comes forth,
> Without erratas, may we think he'll be
> In leaves and covers of eternity.

To complete the parallel it is only fair to quote the famous Franklin variant, which no later elegist has dared try to improve:

THE BODY
of
BENJAMIN FRANKLIN, Printer
(Like the cover of an old book
Its contents torn out,
And stript of its lettering and gilding)
Lies here, food for worms;

Yet the work itself shall not be lost,
For it will (as he believed) appear once more,
In a new
And more beautiful edition,
Corrected and amended
by
THE AUTHOR

Foster's death in 1681 left Boston with a number of booksellers but no printer. The usefulness of a press there had now been shown, and the authorities lost no time in placing it in responsible hands. Another young Harvard man was drafted by the General Court to take over the Foster press, under license, 'and none may presume to set up any other Presse without the like Liberty first granted.' The new incumbent was Samuel Sewall, something of a bookman, an ex-Fellow of Harvard and sometime 'Keeper' of the college library. He had entered the ministry, but he had comfortable 'means,' and preferred the life of a pious layman. Like Foster, he had no knowledge of printing, but could be trusted to keep a Puritan printing house respectable; and he had one of the Greens (another Samuel) to handle the mechanical work. They did official printing for the government and issued some books on their own account. Sewall kept a bookshop, too, one of the first half-dozen in America. But after a few years he began to go up in the political world, lacked time for private business, and was released by the General Court from his duties as manager of the Boston press. Yet busy though he was thereafter as politician, jurist, and man of substance, he kept his touch with the book trade for some time, acting as importer and distributor of books among his acquaintance.

Judge Sewall has come down to us as one of the salient figures of the Puritan period; a personage revered in his time as a pillar of society, and (like Pepys) humanized for posterity by the long-belated publication of his private diary. Unluckily the surviving journals do not cover the strangest phase of his career, during which, for all his realism, he was infected with the madness of the century's closing decade, and helped in the judicial murder of nineteen witches at one assize. This he bitterly repented later, seeking pardon in public meeting for the 'blame and shame' of that judgment. Like Cotton Mather, he outlived the rigor of the Puritan régime and found himself in old age, after nearly forty years' service on the provincial bench, a bewildered spectator of changes that menaced the whole fabric of the colonial edifice. Among other things he was the most diligent book collector of his time. And he was a generous giver of books: 'In the last year of his life he bought and gave away 400 copies of the various publications of the time.'* It is pleasant to think of him as among the first American booksellers.

His printer, Samuel Green the younger, succeeded him in the control of the Boston press. We have an

* Littlefield, 'Early Boston Booksellers.'

engaging miniature of him from the brush of John Dunton: 'I contracted a great friendship for this man; to name his trade will convince the world he was a man of good sense and understanding; he was so facetious and obliging in his conversation that I took a great delight in his company, and made use of his house to while away my melancholy hours.'*
Dunton was a susceptible Briton, and we are not surprised to learn that Green had a wife who was a paragon in a Boston filled with charmers. Both Green and his wife were carried off by the epidemic of smallpox that ravaged the town in 1690.

When Dunton came to Boston the original dynasty in the book world was still regnant. John Usher followed in his father Hezekiah's footsteps, and became a leading citizen: 'He makes the best figure in Boston; he's very rich, adventures much to sea, but has got his estate by bookselling; he proposed to me the buying of my whole venture, but would not agree to my terms; and so we parted with much seeming respect.' So Greek met Greek, without victory or casualty. John Usher continued to be a figure in Boston, was treasurer of the province under Sir Edmund Andros, was absentee lieutenant-governor of New Hampshire for some years; and at last retired from affairs to 'a seat in Charlestown.'

His fellow-Greek John Dunton was one of the most adventurous heroes of the book trade in any period; and since he peddled books in New England for about a year (1786) this chronicle has a fair ex-

* Dunton, 'Life and Errors.'

cuse for telling his tale, especially as his autobiography yields much of what we know of the Boston booksellers of that date. But let us take the story from the learned and urbane Isaiah Thomas: 'John Dunton was born at Graffham, Huntingdonshire, in England; his father was fellow of Trinity College, Cambridge, and Rector of Graffham. Dunton was brought up to the bookselling business in London; where he entered extensively into the trade; and in the course of time became a very considerable publishing bookseller. He had a general correspondence with the booksellers of England, Scotland, Ireland, and Boston. But fortune did not always smile on Dunton. He lost a large sum through becoming surety for his brother-in-law; and was a great sufferer by the troubles of England in 1785, insomuch that his circumstances became embarrassed.' The Monmouth rebellion brought hard times for the book trade. Dunton decided to try his luck in New England with some of his stock. Also the booksellers of Boston owed him £500. 'The management of his affairs in London,' says Thomas, 'he entrusted to his wife, who according to his own account was a most excellent woman, and he had a great affection for her. He embarked on board a ship then lying at Gravesend, and took with him books suitable for the Boston market, to a large amount. He put others to the value of five hundred pounds sterling on board another vessel destined to the same port. The ships were overtaken by foul weather before they cleared the British channel.

That which bore the consignment was lost, but the other, in which Dunton had embarked, weathered the storm. After a tedious passage of nearly four months' duration, he arrived in Boston. Dunton had taken the precaution of procuring letters of recommendation to the most eminent clergymen in Massachusetts, and to the principal gentlemen in Boston; in consequence he was well received and kindly.'* Dunton owns that he was as welcome to the colonial booksellers 'as sour ale in summer. They look upon my gain to be their loss.' But he got himself accepted by the governor and chief officials of the colony, and by the leading clergy, including the Mathers. 'He procured a warehouse, where he exposed his books for sale, and found a good market for them. At the expiration of seven or eight months he had a considerable number of books unsold; but he opened a store in Salem where he soon disposed of the same.'† He sold a good many books to the Harvard College library, John Cotton being then librarian. This amusing 'character' was the first of a long line of English booksellers who found it worth while to bring stocks over here. The books were usually disposed of at wholesale or by auction. Dunton not only set up his own shops, but also did business privately with the local booksellers: 'he that trades with them,' he remarks, with some abatement of his customary cheeriness, 'may get promises enough, but their payments come late.'

* Thomas, 'History of Printing.'
† *Ibid.*

Dunton's account of his first step as a publisher in England is interesting because it describes a practice that goes back to old Rome—a sort of barter or exchange among booksellers, through which their interests were pooled and their stocks built up at small outlay. Dunton's first book was of not much account in itself, but enough to start the ball rolling: 'This book fully answered my end; for exchanging it through the whole trade, it furnished my shop with all sorts of books salable at that time.' This method we shall find persisting among American booksellers well into the nineteenth century. An odd incident of Dunton's stay in Boston was his functioning as joint publisher of the famous Mather sermons on the execution of Morgan the pirate. It was a great occasion—the first hanging in the colony for seven years, and the Revs. Increase and Cotton made the most of it, to the admiration of their flocks. Dunton's partner in this little publishing venture was Joseph Brunning, a Hollander who became one of the leading booksellers and publishers in the colony. Dunton praises him for his fair dealing and especially for his generous attitude toward the wares of others: 'He never decries a Book because 't is not of his own printing; there are some men that will run down the most Elaborate Pieces only because they had none of their Midwifery to bring 'em into public view, and yet shall give the greatest encomiums to the most Nauseous Trash, when they had the hap to be concerned in it. But Brunning was none of these. . . .'

At the time of Dunton's visit, Boston was a town

BOOKSELLING IN BOSTON, 1657-1711   47

of some 5,000 people. Yet within seven years, at about that period, one bookseller imported books to the amount of £567—three or four thousand dollars in modern money. The town cannot have absorbed them all. Hawkers of small wares among the villages sold them with the almanacs and sermons and broadsides of the colonial press. There were other outlets. For all his complaints of business in Boston, Dunton went back to England with his pockets comfortably lined. Times were better at home. He reopened his bookshop on the day the Prince of Orange entered London, and soon built up a new business as publisher and bookseller. Ten years later the wheel had turned again and he found himself almost bankrupt. He had always been, as he confessed, a man of 'rambling and scribbling humours,' with an incurable itch for the pen, though he 'could not stoop so low as to turn author.' Now of his need he sank to that level, in his famous 'Life and Errors of John Dunton, late Citizen of London; Written by Himself in Solitude' (1705). It is a storehouse of information about bookselling and booksellers of his time, including the traders of Boston. Dunton had also to his credit or discredit certain later satires and libels which won him mention and a footnote in the 'Dunciad.'

You don't respect Dunton as you do, for instance, our Isaiah Thomas, but he was a good deal of a 'Figure' in his day, one way and another. As publisher of a whimsical broadside periodical, 'The Athenian Mercury,' in the 1690's, he fairly won place among the London *literati*. Lord Halifax and Sir William Temple commended it; and a young 'Mr. Swift, a country gentleman,' submitted an ode to its editors with an incredibly obsequious letter. A few years later poor Dunton had sunk to a plane far beneath that of the now proud and bitter Dean: from publisher to auctioneer, to butt for Pope and Swift; and at last to a forlorn old age, still scribbling queer comments on his fate. He was sufficiently alive in 1723 to write an appeal to the first George, 'Dying Groans from the Fleet Prison, or Last Shift for Life,' and survived the crisis for another ten years.

Other Boston booksellers of the Dunton period were Richard Wilkins, Samuel Phillips, and Benjamin Harris. Wilkins and Harris were political exiles of the early 1680's. Wilkins is interesting as the first bookseller whose shop is recorded to have been a meeting place for bookish people, as Charles Wiley's became in the New York and the Old Corner Book Store in the Boston of the nineteenth century. Judge Sewall and the Mathers were often there. Wilkins is frequently named in Sewall's journals. He had a good trade. In 1689 he became postmaster of Boston, a position of honor, though there was no domestic mail service at the time and only ships' letters were to be handled.

Another of these Bostonians, Benjamin Harris, made the first colonial attempt to issue a regular periodical: 'Publick Occurences, both Forreign and Domestick.' Like the first English newspaper, pub-

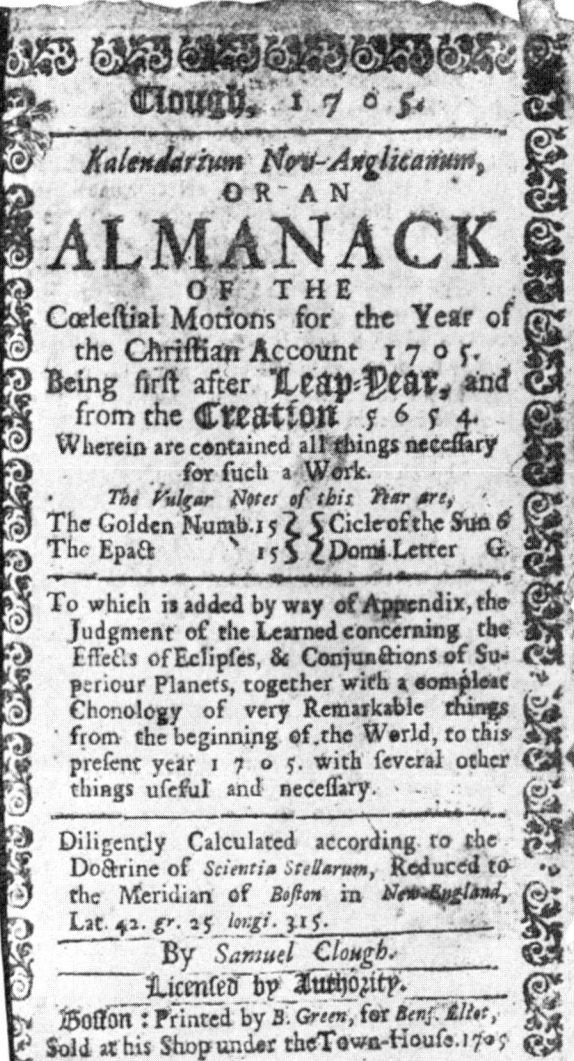

A Typical Eighteenth Century Almanac, Printed by Bartholomew Green.

lished twenty-five years before, it was a folio of two leaves. Harris had kept a bookshop in London and probably had this 'Oxford Gazette' in mind as model. But the colonial government, which was still a Church government also, distrusted so purely secular a publication, through which heretical ideas might be put into the heads of the common people, and suppressed it after a single number. Harris, it seems, was soon forgiven, since two years later he appears as official printer of 'The Acts and Laws of Massachusetts.' Another two years and he had had enough of Boston, went back to England, reopened his shop there, and did well (so far as we know) ever after. Perhaps his excursion to America was to let himself be forgot awhile at home. That seems the implication of Dunton's amiable sketch of Harris: 'He had been a brisk asserter of English liberties, and once printed a book with that very title. He sold a protestant Petition in King Charles's Reign, for which he was fined five pounds; and he was once set in the Pillory, but his wife (like a kind Rib) stood by him to defend her Husband from the Mob. After this (having a deal of Mercury in his natural temper) he travelled to New-England, where he followed Bookselling, and then Coffee selling and then Printing, but continued Ben. Harris still, and is now both Printer and Bookseller in Grace Church Street, as we find by his *London Post,* so that his conversation is general (but never impertinent) and his Wit pliable to all inventions. But yet his Vanity, if he has any, gives no alloy to his Wit, and is no more than might justly spring from conscious virtue; and I do him but justice in this part of his character, for in once traveling with him from Bury Fair, I found him to be the most ingenious and innocent companion that I had ever met with.' Harris, we may think, was the kind of cheerful citizen needed to leaven the rather heavy lump of Puritan New England. Alas, even he did not pass unscathed by the rough satire of the time. According to a couple of scurrilous ballads that have been rescued from oblivion by collectors, his 'kind Rib' was kind to others than her rightful spouse: but this we may fairly take as an invention of political malice.

Samuel Phillips sold books 'At the Brick-Shop at the West-End of the Town-House,' by 1680. He imported a good many books consigned to him by Dunton, who was his 'factor' or agent in London. Dunton commends him as 'very just and (as an effect of that) very thriving. I shall only add to his Character, that he's Young and Witty, and the most Beautiful Man in the Town of Boston.' Pulchritude, male or female, never escaped the rather liquorish eye of old John Dunton. Phillips founded a line of Boston booksellers that continued to do business till after the Revolution. In the chronicles of the time a diverting anecdote connects itself with Phillips by way of his father, the vintner of the tale: 'A Vintner of Boston put up a new Sign called "The Rose & Crown," with two naked boys as supporters. The sight disturbed one Justice S——r, who commanded it down; but the unlucky dog of a carver sent them back two charming Girles. This enraged the Justice more, and the sign was summoned before the wise Court where they gravely determined that the Girles should be encircled with Garlands of Roses.'

Before 1711 there were or had been in Boston, in the neighborhood of the Town House or 'Exchange,' about thirty booksellers. That year came a disastrous fire that seemed to single out the book trade for extinction. It burned the Town House with its little public library, it burned 'all the houses on both sides of Cornhill from School Street to what is called the stone-shop in Dock Square, all the upper part of King Street [later State Street], together with the Town House and what was called the Old Meetinghouse above it.'* Every bookshop in Boston but one went up in smoke. For Boston it was like the 'great fire' of London that had destroyed St Paul's and its cluster of bookshops, forty years earlier.

* Littlefield, 'Early Boston Booksellers.'

IV

PHILADELPHIA AND NEW YORK, *1689-1723*

A VAST deal of literary rubbish must have been disposed of in that Boston fire, as well as many treasures to be lamented by the bibliographer and the collector of Americana. It was a good moment for a clean sweep, if there had to be one. In literature the Restoration period had given England little between the filth of the Rochesters and Etheredges and the sanctimony of Puritan pamphleteers. Congreve and Wycherley, unless by a lighter touch, hardly improved matters. But for Milton, Bunyan, and the best of Dryden, the later seventeenth century had offered little for healthy readers to feed on. Then came purifying influences under Anne: Addison with his clean demure humor, Swift with his savage and cathartic scorn, Pope often ruthless and not always clean, but leading the turbulent roiled stream of English letters between smooth banks and subjecting it to a filter of formal and on the whole salutary taste. The Queen Anne wits were promptly accepted and eagerly bought here. Before the first third of the eighteenth century was over, the colonial versifiers were all imitating the couplets of Pope; and the literary news-weeklies, following the Addisonian pattern, were turning out an urbane and humane trickle of satire and commentary vastly different from the tortured didacticism of the Cottons and the Mathers. Jonathan Edwards was still to come; but his power would be that of a prophet rather than of an official authority. The influence of the ministry, even in its New England strongholds, was on the wane as the eighteenth century came in. The first absorbing business of pioneering was done; the mid-century lapse from culture had been weathered. There were more ease and more money for education and for books. And strict as the religious life of certain sects remained, the Puritan influence no longer ruled unchallenged. A Franklin, not a Mather, would be the dominant personality in eighteenth century America.

With the general loosening or limbering up of society came the rise of private clubs, largely convivial though sometimes dignified with names like the Philosophical Club at Newport and the French Club at Boston: offset by a Beefsteak Club in Philadelphia and a Drunken Club in Maryland. These were informal groups that met, off and on, in taverns and private mansions, and were patterned after the similar clubs and coffee-house gatherings in England—White's and Button's and the Hellfire. These clubs, says Adams, were important 'as focal points for the creating and sharpening of a common consciousness.'* They expressed also a new social cleavage, a

* Adams, 'Provincial Society.'

class consciousness beyond that of the early settlers, for all their ritual of precedence.

Meanwhile the emergence of the newspaper and the magazine gave sign of broadening common interests among a group of colonies hitherto apart from and more or less indifferent to each other. Now New England had lost her monopoly of culture. William and Mary College had risen in the south before Yale in Connecticut or the College of New Jersey, later called Princeton. Presses had been set up in Pennsylvania and New York before the seventeenth century was out. The story of these presses is the story of one man, William Bradford, a salient figure in the history of his trade. He was among the many involuntary missionaries who, cast out of the old country for turbulence or nonconformity, gave sinew to the cultural life of the Western colonies. He was an American 'first' on several counts: the first printer outside Massachusetts, the first in Pennsylvania, the first in New York, the first publisher of a newspaper in New York (as his son was in Philadelphia).

Pennsylvania was chartered by William Penn in 1681. Bradford was among the earliest settlers. He had been apprenticed to a Quaker printer in London, had married his daughter and adopted his faith. By 1686 he had established a printing press 'near Philadelphia,' possibly in Chester (then in Delaware) or in Burlington, N. J. He printed and published an almanac of that date. Its title was 'Kalendarium Pennsylvaniense, or America's Messenger. Being an Almanack for the Year of Grace, 1686. Printed and sold by William Bradford, 1685.' The preface shows how seriously the printer regarded his office: 'Hereby understand,' he adjures the reader, 'that after great Charge and Trouble I have brought the great Art and Mystery of Printing into this part of America, believing it may be of great service to you in several respects, hoping to find encouragement not only in the Almanack, but what else I shall enter upon for use and service of the inhabitants of these parts.' By 1689 he had moved to Philadelphia. He published a number of tracts there shortly after. Two of them were by George Keith, a clever but contentious Scot who became so overbearing in Quaker meeting that he was forbidden to speak there. A faction, including Bradford, sided with him, and Bradford printed his outbursts against a majority headed by the chief officials and magistrates of the province. Silenced by local authority, Keith appealed to a general meeting of the Friends, printed a statement of his case and distributed it among the Quakers before the meeting. The word lobbying seems not to have been invented, but the thing existed, and was a *casus belli* then as now: 'This conduct was highly resented by his opponents; the address was denominated seditious, and Bradford was arrested and imprisoned for printing it.'*

As in Boston at the same time, the civil magistrates of Pennsylvania were also the religious masters of the community. As for freedom of the press, Milton had made his plea for it a few years earlier, but the idea

* Thomas, 'History of Printing.'

had hardly been grasped in England, and would have seemed preposterous in the colony of Massachusetts or Pennsylvania in the year 1690. With Bradford was imprisoned a tailor named John MacComb whose offense was 'in having two copies of the address, which he gave to two friends in compliance with their request.' Bradford petitioned for a hearing, and after some delay was allowed to appear before the magistrates. What followed is worth rehearsing as typical of the court skirmishing, whether in seventeenth century Philadelphia or twentieth century New York, between a defendant who identifies himself with a Cause, and a judge who stands for authority. But for its superior English, the dialogue might be between a modern radical disturber and a police court judge:

"*Justice Cook*. What bold, impudent and confident men are these to stand thus confidently before the Court?

'*MacComb*. You may cause our hats to be taken off, if you please.

'*Bradford*. We are here only to desire that which is the right of every free born English subject, which is speedy justice, and it is strange that that should be accounted impudence, and we impudent fellows therefore, when we have spoke nothing but words of truth and soberness, in requesting that which is our right and which we want; it being greatly to our prejudice to be detained prisoners.

"*Justice Cook*. If thou hadst been in England, thou would have had thy back lashed before now.

'*Bradford.* I do not know wherein I have broke any law so as to incur any such punishment.

"*Justice Jennings.* Thou art very ignorant in the law. Does not thee know that there's a law that every printer shall put his name to the books he prints, or his press is forfeited?

'*Bradford.* I know that there was such a law, and I know when it expired.

"*Justice Cook.* But it is revived again and is in force, and without any regard to the matter of the book, provided that the printer shall put his name to the books he prints, which thou hast not done.'

The prisoners continued to press for a trial.

"*Justice Cook.* A trial thou shalt have, and that to your cost, it may be.'*

Cook was evidently a magnate of the turkey-cock breed; we see him shaking his red wattles in fury at Bradford's impudence. He had the pleasure of sending the prisoner back to jail for some months. At the eventual trial Bradford, who had evidently been mugging up the law, pleaded his own case with great boldness and ingenuity and won it on the technical ground that there was no absolute proof he had printed the offensive pamphlet. He was involved in a similar suit shortly after and fined. His attitude toward Quakerdom became less and less Quakerish. He spoke of the proprietor of the colony as 'my Lord Penn,' and in general flouted the oligarchy on whose favor his living depended. Philadelphia became too hot or too cool for him, and in 1793 he shook her

* Thomas, 'History of Printing.'

dust from his feet and departed for the northern village of New York. The Philadelphia press passed nominally to one Jansen, but he was probably Bradford's agent, and served to hold the little business together till Bradford's son Andrew was old enough to take charge. William may have been a bit chastened by his Philadelphian experience. And in New York he found more freedom, or at least more tolerance. A press was wanted there for official printing. Bradford was appointed government printer, and his first book of the laws of the colony describes him as 'Printer to their Majesties, at the Sign of the Bible.' Bradford seems to have borne himself discreetly in New York, relieving himself by occasional anti-Quaker blasts in the direction of Philadelphia. For more than thirty years he was not only the official printer but the sole printer in New York. To him therefore we shall find Benjamin Franklin, driven out of Boston by his own chicane in the year 1723, naturally turning for employment.

To William Bradford's other distinctions as a 'first' should be added that of being the first paper-maker in the colonies. The almost infallible Isaiah Thomas gives him credit for this, but not enough credit. Thomas says Bradford owned a paper-mill in Elizabethtown, N. J., 'as early as 1728. . . . It is not altogether improbable that it was the first built in British America.' But in 1690 William Bradford was already building a paper-mill near Germantown, which was put in charge of a paper-maker named

Rittenhouse. Two early doggerel-makers who undertook to boost the new colony in its early years sang of this mill. One of them stressed the fact that both linen and paper were made in the Germantown neighborhood:

> One Trade brings in Imployment for another,
> So that we may suppose each Trade a Brother;
> From Linnin Rags good Paper doth derive,
> The first Trade keeps the second Trade alive.*

The other rhymester, a few years later, celebrated Bradford's versatility:

> Here dwelt a printer and I find
> That he can both print books and bind;
> He wants not paper, ink, nor skill,
> He's owner of a paper mill.
> The paper mill is here hardby
> And makes good paper frequently,
> But the printer, as I here tell,
> Is gone unto New York to dwell.
> No doubt but he will lay up bags
> If he can get good store of rags.
> Kind friend, when thy old shift is rent
> Let it to the paper mill be sent.†

The cry of Old Rags grew more insistent as years went by, till at the time of the Revolution it became a wail. Paper was one of the major problems of the

---

* Quoted by Wroth from Richard Frame's 'Short Description of Pennsylvania,' 1692.

† Quoted by Wroth from John Holme's 'True Relation of the Flourishing State of Pennsylvania,' 1696.

colonial printer: 'It is quite likely that paper was more emphatically an immediate cause for the outbreak of the spirit of revolt than the insipid herb of which so much has been written. Certainly one would like to think this true. Tea as the father of the Eagle has always been something of an embarrassment to the American with a sense of humor. Paper is a much more dignified and spiritually important commodity. A tax on paper struck a vital blow at the business of the American printer, and the provincial craftsman was likewise the newspaper editor and a political influence in his community. United, he and his fellows formed a powerful factor in opposition. . . . We hear little of the illegality of taxing paper, but there seems to have been a furious pother about tea. The air was full of tea, and one suspects the printers of having thrown it about to screen their real grievance. Any article of general use would have served their purpose, but they did not want to make paper the test article. They needed paper and they succeeded in having the cheaper grades of the commodity, the newspaper grades, included in the schedule of exceptions in the various non-importing resolutions of 1789.'*

It was then that they began to build up the colonial paper-making industry of which we hear much in the Revolutionary years. Only rag paper was used, and the newspapers were full of appeals for the indispensable commodity. Wroth quotes one

* Wroth, 'Colonial Printer.'

of the most amusing, by Moses Johnson, New Hampshire bookseller and proprietor of 'The Cheshire Advertiser,' (on March 22, 1792): 'Moses Johnson informs all little Misses, and others his Customers, that he receives all kinds of Cotton or Linen Rags and flatters himself they will be encouraged to save them when they are informed 1½ lb. of Rags will buy a Primer or a Story Book, one yard of ribbon, two thimbles, two Rings, twelve good Needles, two strings of Beads, one Penknife, nine rows of Pins—4 lb. will buy a pair of handsome Buckles, or the famous History of Robinson Crusoe, who lived 28 years on an uninhabited Island.' The ingenious Johnson recommends 'Crusoe' not only as an amusing tale, but as nourisher of 'a taste for history of larger extent and importance, such as geography, husbandry, revolutions of countries, &c.' His wants are catholic as well as his wares. He can supply Bibles, spelling books, Watts's 'Hymns' and Morse's 'Geography,' wherefor 'All kinds of Country Produce received at the highest cash price.'

Half a century earlier a versified plea for rags had appeared in the 'Virginia Gazette.' Worthington C. Ford rescued it from a vanished file, and it deserves to be kept as a witty relic of a Southern culture that kept abreast of the best contemporary writing in England. Here is a true product of the age of Pope and Gay, and we may well wish we might know what gentlemanly presence lurked behind the signature 'J. Dumbleton':

> Ye Fair, renowned in Cupid's Field,
> Who fain would tell what Hearts you've killed,
> Each Shift decay'd lay by with care;
> Or Apron rubb'd to bits at—Pray'r.
> One Shift ten Sonnets may contain,
> To gild your Charms and make you vain;
> One Cap a Billet-doux may shape,
> As full of Whim as when a Cap,
> And modest 'Kerchiefs sacred held
> May sing the Breasts they once concealed.
> Nice Delia's Smock which, neat and whole,
> No man durst finger for his Soul,
> Turn'd to Gazette, now all the Town
> May take it up, or smooth it down;
> Whilst Delia may with it dispence
> And no Affront to Innocence.

Till the very edge of the Revolution most of the paper used here, and the best of it in point of quality, continued to be imported from England, but delays in transportation and uncertainty of delivery were so great that a domestic product even of inferior quality was indispensable. Bradford kept a quarter interest in the Germantown mill for a dozen years after he left Philadelphia, taking his profits in paper. Meanwhile through Jansen the printer and later his son Andrew, he continued to milk the cow that had kicked him out of the stall. Franklin sums up William Bradford 'a sly old fox'; and he really seems to have been almost as receptive of the main chance as Yankee-born Benjamin himself. He had staying powers, too, lived to be ninety-four; and on the morning of the day of his death 'walked over a great part of the city.' The 'New York Gazette' gave him an obituary any man might envy: 'He was printer to the government upwards of fifty years; and was a man of great sobriety and industry; a real friend to the poor and needy, and kind and affable to all:—His temperance was exceedingly conspicuous; and he was almost a stranger to sickness all his life. He had left off business several years past, and being quite worn out with old age and labour, his lamp of life went out for want of oil.' A fine fragment of the true poetry to be found in the best of the epitaphs fading from gray headstones in old colonial graveyards.

By 1712 Andrew Bradford was old enough to be sent to Philadelphia in pursuit of an opening for a government printer. He was permitted to bid for the post against a single Philadelphia applicant, and won it. His first job, as usual in all these cases, was to print the laws of the colony. For a full decade he was the only printer in Pennsylvania. He also did bookbinding, and sold books, pamphlets, and almanacs; as well as whalebone, live geese feathers, pickled sturgeon, chocolate, and Spanish snuff. No doubt he would have dispensed cigarettes and sundaes, had those commodities been known. Even down to the nineteenth century it was the booksellers, not the apothecaries, who did that kind of miscellaneous catering. Andrew Bradford was the first colonial book dealer of account outside New

England. His father sold a few pamphlets in New York, and a shadowy Abraham Delanoy is supposed to have dealt in books there about 1700. But New York, illiterate and indifferent, had no considerable bookseller for another forty years. A few boys from the more prosperous families were sent to England or Boston for schooling. There were no local schools. In 1713 a contemporary wrote: 'The city is so conveniently situated for trade and the Genius of the people is so inclined to merchandise, they generally seek no other education for their children than writing and arithmetick. So that letters must be in a manner forced upon them.' The townsmen would appropriate no money for schools. Among six hundred-odd signers of a petition addressed to the King, in 1701, sixty-one had to make their mark. Matters were not much better, we have seen, in rural New England; but in Boston and Philadelphia they were decidedly better. In the South there were a few schools, and more tutors, for the children of the rich whites. Boston with her schools, her printers, and her booksellers, remained the chief cultural centre of the colonies till the eighteenth century was well on its way.

V

THE FRANKLINS

Soon after the fire that burned up most of the Boston bookshops, many of the old dealers were doing business in other quarters; and there was new blood still flowing in from the old country. Thomas Fleet was one of the interesting men of the time. He was born in England, bred a printer, and driven to America by his nonconformist activities. In 1712 he opened a printing shop in Pudding Lane (now Devonshire Street). He printed a few books, many pamphlets, little books for children, and ballads decorated with woodcuts by one of his slaves, who became a clever pressman. Twenty years later, Fleet had handsome quarters in 'Cornhill at the Sign of the Heart and Crown, near the lower end of School Street.' He had a bookshop in the front of his premises, and an auction room where he sold books and also household goods. And from Cornhill, in 1731, he issued one of the first American periodicals modeled after the popular English publications of the 'Spectator' type, 'The Weekly Rehearsal.' Its originator and anonymous 'author' was a clever young gentleman named Gridley, who aspired to be the Addison of the Hub; but he was not encouraged enough, or he tired of the game, for in the course of the year he gave up the experiment and turned the paper over to Fleet, who proceeded to make a successful news-sheet of it, and presently changed its title to 'Evening Post.' It was a weekly of the diminutive type still used at that time in England, a half sheet of foolscap, folio, printed in small pica.

Fleet was a breezy fellow, relished by his townsmen as something of a character. He worked hard, laughed loud, and spoke plain; and he had the knack of enlivening a notice or an advertisement with some quirk of rather hard-boiled humor. As the following: 'To be sold by the Printer of this paper, the very best Negro Woman in this town, who has had the small pox and the measles; is as hearty as a Horse, as brisk as a Bird, and will work like a Beaver.' Pious New England could stomach that, and there is no record of any commotion over a later notice by Fleet offering 'a very valuable Negro woman about thirty years old (sold only for her frequent pregnancy) with a fine healthy boy two years old.' Negroes male and female continued to be among the wares advertised by Yankee booksellers till well toward the Revolution.

No sooner had that new portent the newspaper begun to appear in the colonies than the battle for a free press began. We were not far behind the home country with either the monster or its defence. The British newspaper was only half a century old and had been held by authority to infant proportions and narrow scope, in spite of Milton's trumpet call for liberty. The first successful daily in England came after Anne's accession, 'The Daily Courant,' founded in 1702. Two years later, the Boston postmaster and bookseller, John Campbell, began to publish (as a weekly, to be sure) the 'Boston News-Letter.' It was 'published by authority'; for then and long after, our colonial presses were to be strictly licensed and censored. The irresistible growth of the newspaper in range and importance was confessed when the organ of ephemeral journalism began to call itself and to be called 'the Press,' as if it were now the acknowledged be-all and end-all of the printer's art. At first its performance was feeble enough. The 'Boston News-Letter,' on its half folio sheet of 'pot paper' in small pica, gave a slender dribble of belated news from England, some copied extracts from English papers, and a few items of colonial 'intelligence.' It appealed for advertising, with almost no results. It had but a handful of patrons, and struggled on from year to year pleading for support, threatening discontinuance. Campbell's method was to print what foreign news came to him in the order of its receipt. His space was small, and he was often some months behind with his 'intelligences.' It never occurred to him to scrap his arrearage and start fresh. After fourteen years' struggle, he undertook a sort of supplement, every other week, as a device for catching up. Then he lost the postmastership, his successor took the field with a rival 'Gazette,' and two years later one James Franklin further embarrassed the market with a third weekly, the 'New England Courant.'

This Franklin, whose name has been so thoroughly obscured by his great brother's, is an American worthy of memory on his own account. He was a good printer, a witty journalist, and a bold (not to say impudent) rebel against the Puritan tradition. Though only incidentally a bookseller, he deserves a good place in this chronicle as editor and publisher of the first American periodical of independent character. The 'Courant' had somewhat the status of our 'American Mercury.' It was a journal of nonconformity, and expressed New England's smoldering revolt against the exactions and repressions of the Mather era. For the benefit of the group of clever young fellows who wrote for him, James Franklin kept in the 'Courant' office a small but choice collection of books, including Shakespeare, Milton, Virgil, and other great ones of the past, as well as material more directly to the advantage of his budding satirists: 'Hudibras,' 'The Tale of a Tub,' the 'Spectator' and the 'Guardian.'

Franklin the father had been born in England, and James seems to have served his apprenticeship as printer with family connections in London. When he came home to Boston in 1717 he brought press and types and at once set up for himself. He seems to have done job work for a year or two, then William Brooker, postmaster of Boston, started a second newspaper, the 'Gazette,' to compete with the 'News-Letter' issued by the former postmaster, John Campbell. The connection between the postmastership and journalism was a sort of tradition in the

THE FRANKLINS

colonies for a century or so. The 'Gazette' was passed along with the office for many years. The first change came a few months after its founding, and the new postmaster took the printing away from James Franklin and gave it to Samuel Kneeland, a printer of more experience. This nettled Franklin: he had ideas, anyhow, for a paper of another type, more in the vein of the witty English periodicals, the 'Tatler' and the 'Spectator,' on which young New England (including Benjamin Franklin) was already forming its style. In 1721 James Franklin began to publish the 'Courant' at his own risk. His father and friends advised him against the enterprise; they saw no field for it, with two newspapers already in the colony. He persisted, and the new flavor of the 'Courant' brought it some success. Its news was negligible. Its feature was a short essay each week, done in a mood irreverent of the staid conventions of old Boston, often saucy and always provocative. It attacked magnates in office, and mocked religious orthodoxy and even the clergy. Its essays or leaders were written by a group of men soon damned (and advertised) by respectability as a crew of Free-Thinkers or even as a 'Hell-Fire Club.' The 'News-Letter' and the 'Gazette' of course took the respectable side. The 'Gazette' printed an 'address to the public' by the venerable Increase Mather attacking the 'Courant' as a vile sheet. He marvels that such a publication is tolerated: 'I can well remember when the Civil Government would have taken an effectual Course to suppress such a *Cursed Libel*!

which if it be not done I am afraid that some *Awful Judgment* will come upon this land, and that *the Wrath of God will arise and there will be no remedy*. I cannot but pity poor *Franklin*, who though but a *Young Man* it may be *Speedily* he must appear before the Judgment Seat of God, and what answer will he give for printing things so vile and abominable?'

Poor old prophet, his day is done, his shaking voice merely utters useful publicity for young James Franklin. If the majority of pious citizens still gave assent to the Mather formulas, there was a new and powerful spirit abroad which refused both the dogmas and the prohibitions of the older order. The 'Courant' had its defenders as well as its accusers; and it had the advantage of being readable. It had the honor also of being a nursery and playground for the already skeptical young apprentice Benjamin Franklin. He presently took a hand in the literary impishness of the 'Courant.' And his name appeared for some time as publisher of the sheet, after James Franklin had been forbidden by the authorities to issue it. To use his name, it was necessary to release Benjamin from his indentures of apprenticeship, substituting a private agreement. One piece of sharp practice leads to another: 'At length a new difference arriving between my brother and me, I ventured to take advantage of my liberty, presuming that he would not dare to produce the new contract. It was undoubtedly dishonourable to avail myself of the circumstance, and I reckon this action as one of the first errors of my life.'*

It bore at all events notable consequences for the world. Benjamin, who had as yet no idea of being anything but a printer (unless it were a successful amateur of the Addisonian essay) made straightway for the nearest printing house outside of Boston, which happened to be that of William Bradford in New York. And William Bradford had no job for him but sent him along to Philadelphia where his son Andrew might have room for him. And Benjamin Franklin took root in Philadelphia and did much toward making it for many years a centre of American provincial culture.

Already the Boston apprentice was an eager disciple of the new cult of science or 'Reason.' He fed with avidity on the liberal books now freely imported by colonial booksellers. The Puritan die-hards fought bitterly but in vain. As late as 1713 Cotton Mather tried to get a law enacted restricting the hawkers who distributed books among the farms and villages in the back-country, from dealing in anything but books of piety. It would not do. Franklin as a printer's boy had some special chances; there were booksellers' apprentices of his own age who lent him books on the sly from their masters' stock: 'How often,' says Franklin in the 'Autobiography,' 'has it happened to me to pass the greater part of the night in reading by my bed-side, when the book had been lent me in the evening and was to be returned

* Franklin, 'Autobiography.'

the next morning lest it be missed or wanted!' Also a well-to-do citizen, one of the Adamses, gave him the run of his library. Franklin read Locke and Shaftesbury, took a cubbish delight in being a skeptic, 'and being previously so as to many doctrines of Christianity, I found Socrates's method to be both the safest for myself as well as the most embarrassing to those against whom I employed it. It soon afforded me singular pleasure; I incessantly practiced it; and became very adroit in obtaining, even from persons of superior understanding, concessions of which they did not foresee the consequences. Thus I involved them in difficulties from which they were unable to extricate themselves, and sometimes obtained victories which neither my cause nor my arguments merited.' His brother James, by no means a dull fellow, must have been one of the victims of this method; his childish opponent slily smiling.

James Franklin appears in Franklin's autobiography in an ungratiating light. Isaiah Thomas evidently thinks the younger brother did him injustice. It is clear that a happy relation between these two was impossible. James was twice Benjamin's age, a man of impetuous and irritable temper. Benjamin at twelve was not only his young brother but his apprentice. Benjamin was a cocksure infant who had already developed a natural love of argument by poring over the 'books of religious controversy' of which his father's library largely consisted. The apprentice often argued with the master. 'Our disputes were frequently brought before my father; and either my brother was generally in the wrong or I was the better pleader of the two, for judgment was commonly given in my favor. But my brother was passionate, and often had recourse to blows; a circumstance which I took in very ill part.'* At his worst the author of 'Poor Richard' was capable of a maddening complacency. No wonder the elder retorted with a smack or two when his hireling persisted in being clever at his expense, in his time. James too was clever, a skeptic and a liberal. The differences between the brothers were less intellectual than temperamental; and it was a clash of 'the generations.' It was harsh of James to block all Benjamin's efforts to find an opening among the other printers of Boston. But he had escaped his apprenticeship by a piece of sharp practice, and must be disciplined. Franklin resented this, never quite forgave it, and in old age painted an unflattering and ungenerous picture of his elder brother, long dead. Not that they were active enemies to the end. James Franklin was among the customers recorded in Franklin's famous ledger, for the printers' supplies, especially paper and ink, in which B. Franklin of Philadelphia dealt largely for many years.

Andrew Bradford, when Franklin drifted to Philadelphia in 1723, was a prosperous bookseller but had a very limited printing business outside official work. He had no place for Franklin the journeyman printer from Boston. But he took him into his house

* Franklin, 'Autobiography.'

for a time as a lodger, and found him a job with another printer who had just set up in business in Philadelphia. Samuel Keimer came from London, with a small second-hand equipment. He was a compositor and knew little of presswork. Franklin was a godsend to him, set his press in order, did his presswork, and helped in the small shop where books and pamphlets were sold as well as bayberry candles and Liverpool soap. Keimer printed a few pamphlets and almanacs, but the prospects of advancement in his establishment were small. He was an eccentric and something of a mystic after the French pattern—'enthusiast' was the word. Hardly beyond illiteracy, he loved to turn out verses with a composing stick. He had neither the common sense nor the industry to recommend him to the canny and pushing young New Englander. Already Franklin had his steady eye on the main chance, and had begun to show the genius for human contacts that speeded him so much on his upward way. He made friends at once in Philadelphia, and somehow attracted the notice of Governor Keith of Pennsylvania. Keith urged him to set up a printing business of his own, offered him government patronage, and wrote a letter to Franklin's father urging that he back the enterprise. Benjamin was then but eighteen, and the paternal Franklin had no great cause for confidence in him. He declined to take a hand; whereupon, by Keith's advice, Franklin went to England with the promise of funds to buy printing machines and materials. He was to have also introductions and letters

The Franklins 75

of credit, but Keith seems to have been an ardent maker of promises who seldom fulfilled them. Franklin writes bitterly of him in the 'Autobiography.' The upshot was that Franklin found himself in London without money or friends, and after a year and a half there as a journeyman printer came back to Philadelphia sufficiently humbled to take a job again with the erratic Keimer. During his absence, to be sure, Keimer had come up somewhat in the world. He had faked up a profitable almanac or two, had got hold of some government printing, had moved into better quarters. But it appeared that his expansion had been bold rather than justified. Franklin soon left him, and with money supplied by the father of a fellow-journeyman, Hugh Meredith, he set up as a rival of Keimer and Bradford. To tell the truth, if we accept Isaiah Thomas's account of it all, Franklin played the part of cuckoo in the nest with all these early associates. The new house of Meredith and Franklin soon squeezed Keimer out of the market, took over his new paper, the 'Mercury,' and got the job of government printing. Soon after, Franklin completed his process of edging out the home birds by getting the Philadelphia postmastership away from Andrew Bradford, who had held it for years, and by encouraging Meredith to sell out his share in their business, for £30 and a new saddle.

Isaiah Thomas, it has been hinted, regarded these and kindred proceedings of the young Franklin with a critical eye. He himself had known the great man in his mellow old age; admired him for his achievement but looked on him with something short of worship. In the 'Autobiography' Franklin tells how old William Bradford introduced him to Keimer, and took occasion to find out Keimer's plans without letting him know he was talking to the father of his rival. 'I instantly saw,' says Franklin, 'that one of the two was a cunning old fox, and the other a perfect novice.' It is clear enough which one the philosopher admires in retrospect. Franklin also says that both Bradford and Keimer appeared destitute of every qualification necessary in their profession. Bradford had not been brought up to it, and was very illiterate. Keimer was 'totally ignorant of the world, and a great knave at heart.' Isaiah Thomas quotes some of these phrases and remarks of Keimer: 'It does not appear that he was destitute of all worldly knowledge, but he was unfortunate. He might possibly have been more successful in business, had not his exertions been counteracted by those who, in pecuniary concerns, possessed more sagacity than he did.'

Whatever their quality, it is plain that the Yankee was too much for Bradford and Keimer, and for Meredith also in his turn. Thomas says, 'Franklin soon considered Meredith as a dead weight and was desirous of throwing him off, which he effected with ease.' He had felt himself out by now, and knew what he could do. The debts which bulked so large in his final arrangement with Meredith he was able to discharge in a year or two, and for the next fifteen years he ran his growing business without a

THREE LETTERS

FROM THE REVEREND

Mr. G. WHITEFIELD:

VIZ.

LETTER I. To a Friend in *London*, concerning Archbishop *Tillotson*.

LETTER II. To the same, on the same Subject.

LETTER III. To the Inhabitants of *Maryland*, *Virginia*, *North* and *South-Carolina*, concerning their Negroes.

PHILADELPHIA:
Printed and Sold by B. FRANKLIN, at the *New Printing-Office* near the Market.
M,DCC,XL.

AN EARLY 'FRANKLIN IMPRINT.' A CONTROVERSIAL WORK PUBLISHED FOR HIS FRIEND WHITEFIELD BY FRANKLIN DURING WHITEFIELD'S STAY IN AMERICA.

partner. It was during this time that he became active as a bookseller and publisher. As proprietor and editor of 'The Pennsylvania Gazette,' as compiler and publisher of 'Poor Richard's Almanac,' and as dealer in paper and printer's ink he did a varied and profitable trade. He published an American translation of Cicero by a Philadelphian, and various other books now highly valued for the imprint. In one way and another, by practicing the precepts of Poor Richard and never dropping a stitch of industry or opportunity, he developed a snug business that, when he got ready to enter public life, he could put into the hands of a working partner and virtually retire from with safety. During his partnership with David Hall he continued to draw profits from the business, while Hall did all the work. For some years, according to Thomas, Hall paid Franklin a lump sum of a thousand pounds a year 'as a relinquishment of his share in the profits of the business.' Poor Richard was at last on 'Easy Street'!

The part he played in national and world affairs hardly belongs to a story which regards him as a writer, printer, publisher, and seller of books. He never lost interest in his old trade, and in his last years was at great pains to set up his grandson Benjamin Franklin Bache as a printer and publisher and also as one of the first native type founders—Bache as a boy was trained as a type founder under the famous Didot. Returning to Philadelphia with Bache, Franklin brought a French foundry, and ran it for a year or two while Bache was finishing at college.

For some reason Bache never made much of it, nor is he remembered as a printer and bookseller of the first order. Benjamin Franklin had done what he could toward handing on the torch. For himself he was content to leave intact the famous epitaph, written long before—the epitaph not of a statesman or a philosopher, but of a maker, handler, and lover of books.

Meanwhile during the middle years of his famous brother's career, James Franklin had lived his own life with credit, in his chosen place. Not long after Benjamin Franklin left Boston, the 'Courant' had to be dropped, and its publisher felt the east wind of orthodox opinion. There was another brother in Newport, who now persuaded him of a good opening for a printer in those parts: Rhode Island had none so far. Her intellectual atmosphere was milder, and her authorities encouraged the coming of an experienced printer. In Newport James Franklin set up his press about 1727. He did the usual government printing, and published a pamphlet now and then, and an almanac annually. His first attempt to issue a newspaper failed not for lack of decorum, as his Boston venture had, but for lack of custom. His radicalism had either toned down or was unregarded by the offspring of Roger Williams. He was a citizen useful and well-regarded till his death in 1735. He was born, married, and died on the fourth of February. His widow Anne Franklin succeeded him, and not only carried on the establishment but developed it into a successful business. She did the public printing, and published a number of books and pamphlets by local writers. She carried on the family almanac under the name used by James, 'Poor Robin' (which antedated the 'Poor Richard' of Benjamin Franklin by some years). She wrote her own copy on occasion, when her regular almanac-maker gave out. For a time at least she used as imprint: 'The Widow Franklin at the Town School-House.' She had a son, James Franklin Junior, who was growing up in the trade, apprenticed at his uncle's in Philadelphia. A fine chance for revenge, had Benjamin been malicious, but the nephew came back to Newport unscathed and duly took up the burden of the family press. At least his name was now used, though his mother was probably an active partner. They printed the colony's currency, and in 1758 began to issue the 'Newport Mercury,' which still exists, the oldest American newspaper to be published continuously.

During Anne Franklin's incumbency she had the practical help of her two daughters, who, says Thomas, had been taught by their father to be correct and quick compositors, and were by nature 'sensible and amiable women.' They passed out of the picture presently, we suppose by marriage; but Anne Franklin's work was not done. James her son died in his twenties, and again the mother bent under the yoke. It had grown to be too much for her, and she took on a partner, Samuel Hall. On her death Hall inherited the printing business and the 'Mercury.' But he was not a Rhode Islander, and wishing to live in Salem, he presently sold the Newport concern to a native, Solomon Southwick, a sturdy citizen whose name should be preserved in the annals of his time. He bought Samuel Hall's shop, in 1768, continued the 'Mercury,' and 'published for his own sales several small volumes; but the turbulence of the times checked his progress in this branch of printing.'* He was a stout Whig and edited the 'Mercury' boldly and ably in the interest of the Revolutionary cause. In 1774, when Boston was under a virtual blockade, and the King's troops were quartered there, he appealed to the people of Rhode Island to resent the oppression of the sister colony as 'a direct invasion of the liberties of all the colonies,' and called on them to 'Join or die!' When it came Newport's turn, two years later, to be occupied by the British, Southwick had a narrow escape in an open boat, as a Whig marked for punishment. His houses and property in Newport were destroyed. He was a member of the Rhode Island assembly, and later commissary general of the newly created State. When the British left Newport he returned at once and took up his old trade, and kept going for some years. But he was one of the many patriotic printers and book dealers whom the war ruined. His faith in the wartime paper money cost him dear. He had to sell his 'settlement notes' at the moment of their worst depreciation. 'He was engaged,' says Isaiah Thomas, 'in the cause of his country in the times of her adversity and danger, but he had no portion in the benefits result-

* Thomas, 'History of Printing.'

ing from her prosperity.' He died poor and half-forgotten, just before the century ran out.

Before we leave the Boston neighborhood for awhile, behold Daniel Fowle of that town, a citizen of independent mind and manners who more than once ran foul of authority. He began printing in 1740 with Gamaliel Rogers, as Rogers and Fowle. They did uncommonly good work as printers, and issued various books, some of them at their own risk. They published an 'American Magazine' which ran three years. They started a newspaper, the 'Independent Advertiser,' in 1748. Six years later, after Rogers had retired, Fowle was arrested for printing a political satire called 'The Monster of Monsters' at the expense of the General Court. This pamphlet, like the one that had got William Bradford in trouble with the Philadelphia authorities, sixty years before, bore no imprint. And like Bradford, Fowle tried to baffle prosecution on technical grounds. When he was brought before the House 'the Speaker, holding a copy of the pamphlet in his hand, asked him, "Do you know anything of the printing of this book?" Fowle requested to see it, and it was given him. After examination, he said that it was not of his printing; and that he had not such types in his printing house. The Speaker then asked, "Do you know anything relating to this book?" Fowle requested the decision of the House, whether he was bound to answer the question. No vote was taken, but a few members answered, "Yes." '*

* Thomas, 'History of Printing.'

Fowle then admitted that he had sold some copies, and that it had been printed by his brother Zechariah and a negro pressman belonging to Daniel (his name was Primus, he lived all his life with his master, and was a pressman for fifty years). Zechariah 'possessed a slender constitution.' He now had a convenient 'fit of the cholic' and could not be brought into court. The upshot was that Daniel went to jail for him, was locked up for two days in a cell with a common thief, next door to a condemned murderer, then taken to the keeper's house and told that 'he might go.' But Daniel's dander was up: 'He refused; observing that as he was confined at midnight uncondemned by the law, he desired that the authority which confined, should liberate him, and not thrust him out privily.' So he stayed in jail some days longer, till he learned that his wife was sick with anxiety for him, when he consented to be released. Disgusted, like William Bradford before him, with this tyranny, Fowle moved to New Hampshire, became the first printer in that colony, and published her first newspaper. Bookselling had been part of his business in Boston and undoubtedly remained so in the other colony.

VI

SMALL-TOWN PIONEERS

WE HAVE seen what a close association there was from the beginning among the colonial printers and booksellers. Such families as the Greens, the Bradfords, the Franklins, the Goddards, functioned like dynasties throughout the colonial period, as the Harpers, Wileys, Appletons, and Putnams would function later on. And from the shops of good printers went out fresh initiates in the 'art and mystery' of printing, to colonies and cities that had need of them. So James Franklin went to Newport, and others to Baltimore and New Haven, Charleston and Providence. As a rule the bookseller followed the printer, or rather the printer became bookseller and publisher in the course of his day's work. He published the local laws and legal blanks, the almanacs and news-sheets, and at his office a few books from Boston or London or, later, even a volume or two with his own imprint, could be bought. Let us group together some of the more notable among these small-town makers and vendors of books, before we return to the larger scene, the three-ring show of Boston, New York, and Philadelphia.

There is William Goddard of Providence, New York, Philadelphia, Baltimore, a man who made his share of noise in his day, and whose personality comes down to us with a tang. He was an assertive and ambitious person, for whom the whole range of the colonies was none too large a stage. He made himself felt wherever he went, and is to be recalled more specifically as 'the man who, single-handed and of his own initiative, established the United States Post Office, and who by the exertion of a sort of divinely foolish courage asserted the right of the newspaper to assert itself contrary to the will of the people.'[*] As a printer his lineage was of the best; he was apprenticed to James Parker who had been apprenticed to William Bradford. Goddard opened a printing house in Providence in 1762, his mother Sarah Goddard supplying the capital. He began at once the publication of a 'Providence Gazette and Country Journal.' It had only the 'Newport Mercury' of the Franklins to contend with in the whole colony; but Newport was the larger town and the 'Mercury' had a start of a few years. The 'Gazette' found little support, and the government printing also was in the Franklins' hands. The field was not big enough for an ambitious young fellow like Goddard. After two or three years, as Thomas says demurely, 'he left his printing house &c, in the care of his mother, and sought for himself a more favorable place of residence.' It was after all as much her business as his, and she had no notion of throwing up

[*] Wroth, 'William Goddard and His Friends.'

the sponge. Under her management the Providence press seems to have done better without the male than with him. There she continued and built up the 'Gazette,' and trained her daughter Mary Katherine to the work of printer and editor.

Her restless son found no opening in New York, but presently settled in Philadelphia and contrived to stay there during seven active years. He became editor and part owner of the 'Pennsylvania Chronicle.' His partners were men of substance but Royalists, who for some time forced the 'Chronicle' to an offensive policy toward the Whig party and personnel. Goddard was not a truckler, and the partnership was dissolved: 'A state of hostility ensued, and newspapers, handbills, and pamphlets were filled with ebullitions of their animosity. Goddard endeavored to prevent the re-election of Galloway to a seat in the house of assembly, but failed.'* His enemies, with the aid of certain creditors, were too much for him in the long run, and in 1773 he moved to Baltimore. He again opened a printing shop and started a newspaper, but soon became too active in politics to give his best time to his business, which he left a good deal in the hands of his sister. Goddard's womenfolk were always on hand to pick up his leavings and carry on! This man had little tact and less humor, but was honest and loyal according to his lights. His sympathies were not with the popular party in the pre-Revolutionary years. But when the hour of stress came, he served the national cause while, says Wroth,

* Thomas, 'History of Printing.'

'many former leaders of the popular party were making terms with the British.' Independent he had always been. He was still a loyal colonial when he set out to provide something better than the inefficient British postal service, and from a line of private riders between Philadelphia and Baltimore, developed a service competing with the British colonial system throughout the colonies. It was named the 'Constitutional Post Office' but nicknamed 'Goddard's Post Office.' In 1775 the Continental Congress took it over, and the British line was proscribed in several of the colonies. When the Revolutionary government was formed, Franklin became Postmaster General, and appointed Goddard comptroller of the Post Office. But when Franklin went on his European mission, he arranged that his son-in-law Richard Bache should succeed him as Postmaster General; whereupon Goddard resigned his comptrollership in some dudgeon and returned to Baltimore. He applied patriotically and Rooseveltianly for a lieutenant-colonel's commission in the army. Meanwhile the business of the printing house continued under the management and in the name of his sister. Apparently she edited the 'Maryland Journal,' too, while Goddard had the credit of being its proprietor and director. In 1777 a satirical squib in the 'Journal' offended a 'Whig Club' of prominent Baltimoreans, and when Goddard refused to reveal the name of the author, even under some pressure, they issued an edict in the pure style of klan and vigilante: '*Resolved*, that William Goddard do leave this town by twelve o'clock tomorrow morning and the county in three days. Should he refuse due obedience to this notice, he will be subject to the resentment of a LEGION.'

Goddard promptly carried the matter to the State Assembly, which backed him up and gave him protection. A later ruction of the same kind came to a similar end. Goddard was not a mere hapless victim of persecution. He loved contention and controversy, and his mother vainly wrote him from Providence of the futility of faction and dispute. He fought his fights, enjoyed them, and had his share of victory. In later years he became a considerable bookseller, and made enough money to retire to Providence and marry an Angell. His mother Sarah Goddard had kept up the Providence printing shop and the 'Gazette' for a number of years, latterly with John Carter for partner. Carter had been an apprentice of Franklin's in Philadelphia. For twenty years he continued as a printer and bookseller, 'At Shakespeare's Head, opposite the Court House'; most of the time he was serving as postmaster of Providence.

Mary Katherine Goddard, when in control of the 'Maryland Journal' at the beginning of the Revolution, had also acted as postmistress of Baltimore for a time. She was a woman of marked ability and character, did a good deal of business under her own name, and was able to stand up to her temperamental brother at a pinch. She was, says Wroth, 'one of the most conspicuously useful women of her generation in the public life of the nation.'* The Goddards were not the first printers in Maryland. An Englishman, William Parks, had come there from Shropshire in 1719. Up to that time the official printing for the colony had been done by Andrew Bradford in Philadelphia. Parks settled first at Annapolis and became government printer. Later he had a press at Williamsburg. He was founder and editor of a Maryland and later of a Virginia 'Gazette.' He published and sold the usual local and practical matter, but was interested in literature also—a rare thing then—and issued a number of books of colonial verse. He was a practical man, too, and built the first papermill north of Philadelphia.

Among other early printer-publishers in the colonies south of New England was Louis Timothée, a French Huguenot who had learned printing in Holland, came as a refugee to Philadelphia, and found work in Franklin's printing shop. When death offered a vacancy for a printer at Charleston in 1733, he moved there, changing his name to Lewis Timothy. He followed the familiar routine, served as government printer, founded a newspaper that survived throughout the century, and died in 1738. He is looked on as one of the master-printers of the colonial period. His craft did not die with him. The business was carried on at first by his widow and his son Peter, then by Peter alone. Their 'South Carolina Gazette' was the leading newspaper in the colony. It

* Wroth, 'Colonial Printer.'

bore the King's arms and did its best to give the news from the other colonies and from abroad. One thing was as difficult as the other; there was as yet no mail service between the northern and southern colonies. The 'Gazette' depended on the irregular arrival of news by sea. 'The publisher often waited several days for arrivals; but the "Gazette," dated Monday, was always issued within the week.'

Peter Timothy was a man of independent character. A year after he took over the 'Gazette' and the government printing, he risked his standing by printing a letter of one Hugh Bryan which asserted baldly 'that the Clergy of South Carolina broke their Canons daily.' To attack the Church of England in the South was like attacking the Quakers in Philadelphia or the Congregationalists in Boston. Timothy was promptly arrested, in the very distinguished company of George Whitefield the prophet of dissent. Whitefield was then making one of his whirlwind tours of the American colonies, carrying all before him—except the Church of England cohorts. Bryan seems to have been a henchman, and Whitefield was known to have 'corrected' his letter for publication. All three were arrested, but it was only a gesture—or, it may be, Whitefield's popularity warned the authorities not to press the matter beyond what was in effect an official protest. They were all admitted to bail and the case was never brought into court. Peter Timothy kept his job as government printer, and after the Revolution as printer to the State. He served for some years as clerk to the General Assembly. He stayed in Charleston during its siege and capture, became a prisoner of the British, was exchanged, embarked for Antigua where he had a widowed daughter, and was drowned off the Capes of Delaware. His widow, Anne Timothy, carried on, edited the 'Gazette,' printed for the State until her death in 1792. The 'Gazette' continued to be published till 1800 by her son Benjamin Franklin Timothy.

In 1772 Peter Timothy had taken as partner the foreman of his printing house, Thomas Powell. Powell was a man of cultivation and good manners, as well as of ability in his trade. Timothy became silent partner of the firm of Powell and Company. He still edited the 'Gazette' and was active in the firm. But when the 'Gazette' presently offended, Powell was the one to be brought to book. The offence was one that repeatedly got the press into trouble, throughout the colonial period, both in England and here. The 'Gazette' had printed, as news, part of the proceedings of the House of Assembly, the upper house in the colonial government. Powell's sufficient excuse was that 'the copy of the matter there printed was delivered to him by the Hon. William Henry Drayton, one of the members of the house, who desired him to print the same.' The House thereupon judged him guilty of contempt for printing part of their proceedings 'without their order or leave.' No action was taken against the Hon. Mr. Drayton, though he faced the music nobly, as Isaiah Thomas's account shows:

Small-Town Pioneers 91

'Powell was told to ask pardon; he declined. The house then ordered him to be taken into the custody of the sergeant of arms, and brought to the bar. This was done; and when at the bar, he was again informed of the charge against him, and that the house desired to hear what he could say in exculpation of that charge. Powell declared that "he did not know he had committed any offence."

'The Hon. Mr. Drayton in his place acknowledged that he was the person who sent the copy of that part of the journals printed by Powell, to the press, but without intention to offend the house, &c.'

The House, ignoring this, again pronounced that Thomas Powell, 'this day adjudged to have been guilty of a high breach of privilege, and a contempt of this house, be for his said offence committed to the common gaol of Charleston.' Mr. Drayton entered his protest and dissent, but the warrant was issued and Powell went to jail. A few days later he was released on a writ of habeas corpus, brought by the Speaker of the Lower House. The same day Powell issued an extra number of the 'Gazette,' citing Drayton's dissent and protest against the verdict. And now the battle was on. There were political rivalries between the upper and lower houses of the government, the prestige of both houses was at stake. If truncheons could not be used, hairs could be split. The Council of the Upper House at once pronounced that the 'Gazette's' account of the Drayton protest was 'materially different' from the record, and therefore 'false, scandalous, and malicious, tending to reflect upon the honor and justice of the House.' And the Council, which had winked once, now recognized 'that William Henry Drayton was instrumental in the publication.' Drayton at once dissented to the effect that, but for one word and a few misspellings, the 'Gazette's' record was the same as the original. The Council thereupon lost patience with Drayton and charged him with contempt 'in being instrumental to the publication of the protest,' etc. Drayton again dissented and protested, but this was his last sputter. The House voted him in contempt, and he 'purged himself' by a technical manoeuvre. The House then pronounced that the justices who had released Powell were in contempt, and that by their action 'they had, so far as in them lay, absolutely and actually abolished one of the branches of the legislature.' It was now a very pretty quarrel, involving the relations of the two branches of government, with an address to the lieutenant-governor of the colony, and another to the King. But the lower or 'commons' house of assembly at once justified the action of their Speaker, and made their own representations of the case to His Majesty in London. The case was still unsettled when the war began; whereupon it was lost sight of forever, as well as the printer Powell, of whose subsequent fate nothing is known.

A special and important printing and publishing interest in the South up to the Revolution was the result of an immense immigration of Germans, chiefly to Pennsylvania. The first comers were immediate victims of the Thirty Years' War, but the movement continued till, within the half-century between 1683 and 1730, some twenty thousand Germans had settled here. Their story is one of the most malodorous in the colonial record. Colonial agents induced them to come over here, by extravagant promises, herded them into ships where they died like flies, and made virtual slaves of the survivors. Maryland as well as Pennsylvania was guilty of this traffic: the African slave-trade was in no way more barbarous, except that the white victims' slavery was not hereditary. There may have been thirty thousand German-speaking people in Pennsylvania when the first German press was set up there in 1735. The owner and printer was Christopher Sauer, or Sower, 'a man,' says Thomas, 'of good information, and a well-instructed printer.' He was also a writer of some ability. Before long he was issuing a regular newspaper in German as well as almanacs and lesser matter. He got out a German digest of the colonial laws, and printed a great German Bible in 1743.

Soon afterward, his son Christopher Sower the second took over the concern, expanded it steadily, and published and printed many books. He did a large business with later editions of the Sower Bible. At the beginning of the Revolutionary period, 'his was by far the most extensive book manufactory then, and for many years afterward, in the British American colonies. It occasioned the establishment of several binderies, a paper mill, and a foundry for

English and German types.'* Meanwhile Sower's constituency was being surely though slowly assimilated, and the Sower bookshop was disturbed to find more demand for books in English than in German. The Sower property was cruelly dealt with during the Revolution, particularly during the battle at Germantown where the main plant was. Guessing that the British would come out on top, the Sowers took what printing equipment they could to Philadelphia and stayed there during the British occupation. Christopher Sower the third left the country with the British army, settled in New Brunswick, and published a 'Royal Gazette' there. His Pennsylvania estate was confiscated and his stock sold, some of the Bibles in sheets being 'converted into cartridges, and thus used not for the salvation of men's souls, but for the destruction of their bodies.'

Another German, John Peter Zenger, had become a colonial printer about a decade before the first Christopher Sower set up his German press at Germantown. Zenger, however, had no idea of perpetuating his native language here, but wrote and printed English. As a boy he came over with his family in 1710, was shortly apprenticed to William Bradford, and later became his partner for a year or two. He then set up for himself as printer and, before long, was editor of the second newspaper in New York, the 'Weekly Journal.' Thomas says that Zenger was well educated and a good printer, but inaccurate in his command of English. He was a man of firm opinions

* Thomas, 'History of Printing.'

and blunt speech. The origin of his 'Journal' was frankly political. It was an opposition paper from the first, directly pitted against Bradford's 'Gazette,' the administration organ. For Bradford, forty years back a nonconformist and malcontent in Philadelphia, had long since gone over to the side of constituted authority. Soon Zenger's 'Journal' was openly attacking the administration of Governor Crosby and his successor. The assailant seems to have had the moral and perhaps the material backing of the Honorable Rip Van Dam, chief opponent of the Crosby party. Zenger printed various articles boldly attacking the Governor and his policies. About a year after the 'Journal' was started he was arrested on a warrant from the Governor and his Council 'for printing and publishing several seditious libels,' the articles being specified. It was at once recognized as a test case. The House of Representatives refused to concur in the prosecution. The Governor ordered the Mayor of New York to have the libelous papers publicly burned 'by the common hangman, or whipper.' The Mayor ignored the order, and the Governor had the papers burnt by a State officer. A grand jury refused to indict Zenger. The Attorney General was ordered to file an 'information' against him for printing the libels. Meanwhile time dragged on, and Zenger stayed in prison, as he could not get the large bail demanded. Various obstacles were put in the way of his legal defence, and when the trial came it took a Philadelphia lawyer, one Andrew Hamilton, to win the case for the defendant. The jury's verdict of not guilty was received with loud cheers; Mr. Hamilton was rewarded by the Corporation with a grant of the freedom of the city, enclosed in a gold box suitably inscribed. The case established the right of the press to print matter unfriendly to the political power that might happen to possess the upper hand—which is what democracy means by 'the Government.' It brought to a head the question of the freedom of the press. Livingston Rutherfurd says, 'The trial of Zenger first established in North America the principle that in prosecution for libel the jury were the judges of both the law and the facts. The liberty of the press was secure from assault and the people became equipped with the most powerful weapon for successfully combating the conduct of public men, more than fifty years before the celebrated trial of "Junius" gave the same privilege to the people of England.'* This privilege was all very well as a weapon of the people, but in time the press abused it, and it was necessary for a great national figure like Fenimore Cooper to sacrifice ease and popularity in order to establish the limits of liberty and license for the public press. Zenger did his share of the publishing and bookselling of his place and time. After his death his widow Catherine Zenger continued the business in her own name till her son John Zenger Jr. was old enough to take it over. Does this obituary item become monotonous? Truth must be told!

In the course of the eighteenth century there were

* Rutherfurd, 'John Peter Zenger.'

about fifty towns which produced books and newspapers in German. In New York, still largely Dutch in manners and speech, there was a good deal of publishing in Dutch. Elsewhere the Huguenot colonists, many of them persons of cultivation beyond the standard of the British colonials, kept up a demand for books in their native tongue. A catalogue of the French firm of Moreau St. Mery, issued in Philadelphia in 1795, lists nearly a thousand French titles, as well as books in Latin, Italian, Spanish, German, and Dutch: a fair indication that our leading city of that time was quite as cosmopolitan and cultured as our leading city of this time.

VII

BOOKSELLERS OF THE REVOLUTION: NEW YORK

JAMES TRUSLOW ADAMS and others have stressed the individual isolation of the colonies up to the middle of the eighteenth century, the difficulties of travel from one to another, and the almost total lack of communication among them; so that Virginia, for example, was long closer to England than to New England, in all matters connected with current happenings and ideas. Possibly this condition has been exaggerated. Quite early in the eighteenth century we find printers and printers' apprentices passing freely from Massachusetts to New York, from Philadelphia to Pennsylvania, Connecticut, or Virginia. They seem to have been among the most important instruments of liaison. They did much to nourish a common feeling and a common culture among the Yankees and Quakers and Southern planters who, before the century ran out, would find it possible to unite in a common cause and would thus presently (and surprisingly) find themselves bound together as a nation. William Bradford, we have seen, practiced his bookmaking and bookselling trade in Pennsylvania, New York, and New Jersey. James Franklin moved from Massachusetts to Rhode Island, Benjamin Franklin from Boston to Pennsylvania. Goddard fought on every front, from Providence to Baltimore. The readiness with which these men set up their shops in one colony or another and started newspapers offhand that were acceptable to their hosts and customers, shows there was no essential difference between the needs and tastes of a Rhode Islander, a New Yorker, or a Virginian. And the itinerant journeyman printer served as a lesser envoy between colony and colony.

James Parker and John Holt are striking exemplars of the eighteenth century bookseller's mobility and versatility. Parker was apprenticed to William Bradford in New York, in 1725. He ran away, was advertised for (rewards for missing apprentices and runaway slaves were equally common in the newspapers of that period) and came back to serve out his term. He became Bradford's successor in 1742, started the third New York paper, the 'Weekly Post-Boy,' and published the usual run of almanacs, books, and pamphlets. In 1751 he founded the first printing shop in New Jersey. Three years later we find him established as printer and postmaster in New Haven, acting in both functions by deputy. His business grew steadily, and for some time he was the most important publisher in the colonies. He was an independent person, and none too cautious about what appeared in his newspaper, being twice arrested for printing libelous matter. He became one of New York's prominent citizens, was captain of a troop of horse; was, perhaps, not beyond criticism in all respects. At all events there is a cryptic touch to a note that appeared in a New York paper on his death: 'He has left a fair character, on which we have neither time nor room to enlarge.' He had, in a deathbed mood, none too good an opinion of himself. His last will began: 'In the name of God, amen. I, James Parker of the city of New York, reflecting on the uncertainty of this life and being in sound mind and memory blessed be God, do make this my last will and testament as follows: Imprimis: My soul an immortal part not so properly my own as another's, believing it to be purchased by the Lord Jesus Christ at the inestimable price of his own blood, I bequeathe to Him, relying firmly that for his own name and word's sake he will fulfil his promise and fight against the malice of the evil one who by his continual attacks on my poor intellectuals has caused me to be defiled from the crown of my head to the soles of my feet so that I am unable to help myself.'

Connected with Parker's story is the rather odd one of John Holt. He was a Virginian who became a bookseller and journalist first in Connecticut and later in New York. What brought him north in the first place is a mystery. He was a man of good education, a merchant in his native town of Williamsburg who had served as mayor there. But in 1754 we find him deputy postmaster for James Parker in New Haven, and partner and manager in the bookselling and printing business there. Holt edited the 'Connecticut Gazette,' the first newspaper in that colony. Parker had gone back to New York and left him in charge. Holt did so well that he was presently called to New York to take charge of the Parker printing office there. In 1764 Parker retired, or at least the partnership was dissolved, and Holt took over the New York concern. For awhile he carried on the 'New York Gazette' for Parker, but later dropped it in favor of a paper of his own, the 'Journal.' About 1770 he established a printing shop at Norfolk, Virginia, under the management of his son John. This plant was destroyed by Lord Drummond five years later. Holt's 'New York Journal,' unlike the rival sheets of Rivington and Gaine, was strongly and consistently Whiggish during the years before the Revolution. In 1774 he replaced the royal arms on the 'Journal' with Franklin's design of the divided snake, with its provocative motto 'Join or Die.' When the British took New York, his property had to be abandoned there, a total loss. But he managed to carry on the 'Journal,' at first in Esopus and later at Poughkeepsie. He brought it back to the city after the evacuation of the enemy, but died a year later. His widow (another widow!) kept up the business and the paper for some years. Speaking of distinguished colonial booksellers, we should note that at New Haven, in Holt's time or just after it, books (and drugs) were being sold in the shop of a native son of Connecticut named Benedict Arnold.

During their later years, consciously and unconsciously, the colonies had traveled far from the early conditions and the pioneer mood. Loyal in theory to the home country, if not always to the home government, they were steadily developing a civilization or culture of their own. There were the social clubs, and the continual pamphleteering; and the magazines, which for all their crudity marked a step forward from the unicellular literature of the almanac. By mid-century, at least in the central and southern colonies, concerts and the theatre were encouraged and patronized. Well-known English actors like the Hallams toured the country south of the New England deadline. Copley and Benjamin West emerged as artists who were accepted as equals of the British: West was head of the British Royal Academy for many years. The idea of the public library was developed here, before it had been seriously thought of abroad. There were a score and more of them in the colonies before the Revolution.

And while this general process of social and intellectual development was going on, causes of political unrest and conflict were multiplying. The approach of the Revolution found printers and booksellers fairly well divided on the growing issue. Many of them hesitated to take sides till taking sides was a necessity. Some of them made their decisions by guesswork. But most of them were honest on one side or the other, and a surprising number chose what for a long time seemed almost hopelessly the rôle of the under dog. But there were exultant Tories like James Rivington and straddlers like Hugh Gaine. These two New York rivals, playing their game under the precarious conditions of that time, present an amusing if not altogether edifying contrast, both as men and as pawns in the larger play.

Hugh Gaine was a Scotch-Irishman who was born and served his apprenticeship in Belfast, came to New York in 1745 and worked under James Parker. Seven years later he had started a bookselling and stationer's shop. An advertisement of Gaine's in Parker's 'Gazette' in 1752 offers Bibles, prayer books, Church and meeting psalm books, a 'History of the Five Indian Nations,' an 'Account of the Earthquake at Lima,' Ovid and Virgil in the Latin, mariner's compasses, writing-paper, 'also choice good bonnet-papers.' Two months later Gaine was issuing his own newspaper, the 'Mercury,' published at his printing-office, where he advertises 'printing done at a reasonable rate, with care and expedition.' From the beginning he was an assiduous advertiser and horn-blower, far ahead of his time. He was too enterprising for the age in one or two other directions, being reprimanded by the New York Assembly soon after the 'Mercury' was started, for printing some of the proceedings of that house. For a year or two he did little publishing beyond his newspaper and an almanac; but already he was importing a good many books from England; he was still more bookseller than printer. But in time his colophon became familiar: 'Printed by H. Gaine, at the Bible and Crown in Queen Street.' And still later his press was 'the most prolific of its time in New York.'

By the time of the Revolution there were probably fifty thousand Scotch-Irish in the colonies. Most of them were Presbyterians, but Hugh Gaine for some reason was an Episcopalian. His 'Mercury' became the mouthpiece of the Church people in New York, as opposed to the anti-Church element which spoke through Parker's 'Gazette.' It was not long before Gaine was personally vilified by the partisans of Presbyterianism for having turned Churchman in order to ingratiate himself with the ruling class in New York. And he was assailed not only as a turncoat and timeserver but as a liar and coward. Those were plainspoken days, and no words were minced on either side. Gaine's chief enemy was presently careless enough to crib some of his periods from Addison. Gaine at once spotted him and held him up to ridicule as a shameless plagiarist. During the ensuing fracas Gaine printed a number of pamphlets by disputants on his side of the controversy. But it was his instinct to hedge, and he later (for a consideration) gave space to the Presbyterians in a department of the 'Mercury,' and did quite a bit of printing for them, sermons and the like. Gaine was very much on the spot during the French and Indian wars. He imported or reprinted various works on the art of warfare. An advertisement of the period lists broadswords and other properties of war, as well as pomice boxes, razors, Irish butter, boots, and flutes. Later he carried a full line of patent medicines. He prospered, advertised for a housekeeper, presently acquired that cheaper commodity a wife. He discontinued the 'Mercury' at the time of the Stamp Act, but resumed it later, and stood so well with authority as to land (1768) the profitable job of printer to the colony as well as to the city of New York. He was now trying his best to keep his paper unbiased. Under the stress of the coming conflict, this could not long be done. During the early phases of the Revolutionary movement he clearly leaned to the American cause. He printed a good deal of matter on the Revolutionary side, and declined much Royalist matter, but was not zealous enough for the zealots. Still, when Rivington's presses were destroyed in 1775, Gaine's were spared. In 1776 Gaine was still trying to be impartial in his journalism. He advertised Paine's 'Common Sense,' but printed both attacks upon and defences of that famous pamphlet. When the Battle of Brooklyn was lost and the British took New York, it was no longer possible to stay on the fence. Gaine chose the American side and moved his office and some of his presses to Newark where he published several numbers of the 'Gazette.' He was encouraged by New Jersey patriots, including Governor Livingston: 'The times were too much, however, for the printer. Subscribers were in arrears and scattered, new supplies of paper were not obtainable. Worse still, it was quickly evident that the British intended an invasion of New Jersey, and equally certain that the Continental forces under Washington could not prevent their overrunning the state. Even to the most hopeful it seemed that the Continental cause was lost. Threatened with another enforced removal, Gaine abandoned his attempt to print a Whig paper, and . . . returned to New York.'*

Meanwhile the British authorities had taken over Gaine's plant, his newspaper, and even his imprint. One number of the 'Gazette' appeared as 'Printed by Hugh Gaine, Printer, Bookseller, and Stationer, at the Bible and Crown, in Hanover-Square.' Within two months Gaine was back at the old stand, publishing at the Bible and Crown. He had come to terms with the British authorities and presumably with his own conscience, since from that time to the end of the war he appears as a consistent Royalist, in his private as well as in his public journals. By Whigs and patriots he was of course denounced as an apostate, and he suffered the fate of turncoats. The party to which he had turned did not highly trust him. Rivington, an impeccable Royalist, had but to return to New York (in 1777) to be encouraged in the publication of a rival 'Gazette,' and to be given the valuable office of 'Printer to His Majesty.' When the War ended with the Continentals victorious, Gaine found himself in the awkward position of thousands of people who had assumed that the other side would win. In his new-found zeal he had done some of those extreme things with which sudden converts are wont to damn themselves in the eyes of reasonable men. In June, 1777 (at about the time of Rivington's appointment), Gaine's 'Gazette' had asserted that 'the flower of Mr. Washington's Army is composed of the Gleanings of British Prisons, trans-

* Ford, 'Hugh Gaine.'

Booksellers of the Revolution

ported to the Southern Colonies.' And that same year Gaine printed the 'Military Collections and Remarks' of a British major named Donkin, a few copies of which were allowed to go out with the footnote, 'Dip arrows in matter of small pox, and twang them at the American rebels in order to inoculate them; this would sooner disband these stubborn, ignorant enthusiastic savages than any other compulsive measures. Such is their dread and fear of that disorder!'

Naturally the Whig press assailed him as a prize traitor and liar, and it cannot have been an easy berth at the Bible and Crown when the British left New York and its shivering Tories. Gaine at least stuck to his post, trimming his course to the extent of removing the Crown from his imprint, publishing thereafter 'At the Bible in Hanover Square.' There is a tradition that he petitioned the New York Assembly to be allowed to remain in the State, but no record of this can be found except in the lines of Freneau, which purport to be a parody of Gaine's petition. So the ardent poet of the Revolution ensured the printer a certain fame by embalming him in a lively bit of verse which, critically savored, is not much above doggerel. It represents Gaine as an Irish-American adventurer, half impudent and half obsequious, who at the beginning of the Revolution shouted for the Whig cause and used his 'Gazette' to advance it, even 'printing some treason for Philip Freneau.' But when the British fleet came, and Washington retreated from Long Island,

> Like the rest of the dunces I mounted my steed,
> And galloped away with incredible speed.
> To *Newark* I hastened—but trouble and care
> Got up on the crupper and followed me there!
> There I scarcely got fuel to keep myself warm,
> And scarcely found spirits to weather the storm;
> And was quickly convinced there was nothing to do
> (The Whigs were in arms and my readers were few).
> So after remaining one cold winter season
> And stuffing my papers with something like treason,
> And meeting misfortunes and endless disasters,
> And forc'd to submit to a hundred new masters,
> I thought it more prudent to hold to the one—
> And (after repenting of what I had done,
> And cursing my folly and idle pursuits)
> Returned to the city and hung up my boots.

The petitioner admits that he has picked the wrong winner. He is shown sneaking back to New York under cover of night, going to a Tory parson for protection, recanting his errors: 'And so they restored me to Printing and Place.' But he has to serve in the militia and to perform menial duties, while his rival Rivington, exempt as King's printer,

> . . . Laughs till his sides are ready to split,
> With his jest and his satires, and sayings of wit.

All in vain, these penances and humiliations! His British masters have been mastered. And now the printer begs to be allowed to turn his coat again—anything to stay in New York:

My press, that has called you (as tyranny drove her)
Rogues, rebels and rascals, a thousand times over,
Shall be at your service by day and by night,
To publish whate'er you think proper to write;
Those types that have rais'd George the Third to the level
With angels—shall prove him as black as the Devil. . . .

Rough treatment! Freneau the unflinching patriot was also a rival journalist, editor of the 'Freeman's Journal,' in which this satire was printed in January, 1783, some months before peace with England was finally confirmed. Probably the whole thing was an invention. An extant diary of Gaine's ends a few days before Freneau's skit appears, and nowhere hints that the diarist is in any difficulty. The final entry still speaks of the British Fleet as 'our Fleet, bound to England.' New York was not evacuated till Nov. 23, 1783, when (and not till then, according to Ford) Gaine discontinued his 'Gazette.' A comparison of Gaine's laconic diary entries and the news as published in the 'Gazette' shows that paper definitely edited in the interest of British propaganda rather than of military facts. Gaine must be taken as a journalist, and his ethics are those of his tribe. He was a political trimmer till he had to take sides, and then he took his sides tandem—as many another journalist has done under like conditions.

Freneau had had direct contact with Gaine, who published his 'General Gage's Confession' in 1775, and who may have printed his broadside on 'James Rivington, His Life and Death,' that same year. One way and another, as printer, journalist, and publisher, Gaine was a well-known figure in his day, and that day lasted long after the war that had made his position so precarious for a time. The bibliography of his publications is imposing in bulk and more than respectable in content. Besides his weekly 'Mercury' (later the 'Gazette') he produced his full share of the almanacs, calendars, and political pamphlets of the time, and reprinted many of the British eighteenth century classics, Addison's 'Cato,' Blair's 'Grave'; Isaac Watts was a great standby with him. But his highest service no doubt was as bookseller and importer. A single list of 1754, of 'Books just imported from London and to be sold by H.Gaine, at the Printing-Office, between the Fly and Meal-Markets,' gives, besides whole classes of Bibles, prayer books, and grammars, more than a hundred titles of books of science, travel, philosophy, as well as editions of Addison, Defoe, Dryden, Gay, Johnson, Locke, Milton, Pope, Richardson, Thomson, and Young. The list also offers 'Primmers by the Dozen, as well as stationery of all sorts, Pounce and Pounce-Boxes, Spectacles, quills, and bills of sale'; and a runaway slave, and 'To be Sold, a likely NEGRO BOY, about 16 Years of Age. Enquire at the Printer hereof.'

So, for all his shaky past, Hugh Gaine prospered; continued to be an active printer till 1800, dealt profitably in New York real estate, and when he died in 1807, left a good deal of property to his two daughters. His only son had died young.

James Rivington, Gaine's chief rival, comes down to us almost as vivid a figure as Gaine himself. He was the second son of the Charles Rivington, founder of the famous London publishing house, who had begun business by buying out Richard Chiswell, publisher of the Shakespeare Fourth Folio. John the elder stayed with his father and carried on the line. James, 'bred a bookseller,' set up for himself early in life, made money, got into smart and fast company, went bankrupt, and came to America to turn over a new leaf about 1760. The English Rivingtons were staunch Church and King men, and James stood by the family tradition. He had large views in business, for the times, and in a couple of years was settled in New York as bookseller, with branches or agencies in Philadelphia and Boston. Perhaps he overrated his market for the large stocks of books he imported from England. He failed in business, and took to printing. In 1773 he started a Tory newspaper, the 'New York Gazetteer,' which took the King's side so strongly that at the end of 1775 a band of Connecticut Whigs raided the city, broke into his printing house, ruined his press, and carried off his types to melt down into good Whig bullets. Soon after, Rivington got a new press from England and was appointed King's Printer for New York. His 'Royal Gazette,' issued during the British occupation of the city, became notorious for its propagandist news of the war, and when after the peace Rivington stripped it of its royal title and emblems and tried to carry it on as 'Rivington's New York Gazette,' there was no public to support it, and it died unlamented.

Rivington like Gaine became a butt for the chorus of satirical rhymers who suddenly sounded, like peep-frogs in Spring, at the dawn of the new republic. His 'Gazette' in its Royal days had printed Tory satires, including their poet laureate's masterpiece, Jonathan Odell's 'The Congratulation.' Now triumphant patriots were delighted to see the Britisher withdrawing the symbols of royal pride and trying to pass himself off as an American citizen. Freneau's travesty of Hugh Gaine's alleged petition was paralleled in 'Rivington's Confessions, Addressed to the Whigs of New-York.' Rivington was a person far more polished than Gaine, and affected the manners of an elegant and convivial gentleman:

Long life and low spirits were never my choice,
As long as I live I intend to rejoice;
When life is worn out, and no wine's to be had,
'T is time enough then to be serious and sad.

Now, rather jauntily, he pleads himself a repentant sinner, 'sick of the scarlet and slaves of the throne,' and ready to 'adore the daystar'! At least he has not been willing to fly with the redcoat rabble, and may reasonably ask leave to remain in the city of his choice:

I hope while I live you will all think it best
To allow me to bustle along with the rest.
A view of my life, though some parts might be
    solemn,
Would make on the whole a ridiculous volume.
In the life that's hereafter (to speak with submission)
I hope I shall publish a better edition.

And a Rev. Mr. Witherspoon of Philadelphia thought Rivington worth a long prose 'Supplication of J— R—— to Congress,' in which the humors and squalors of his recantation are heavily labored. It is clear that Gaine and Rivington, as leading booksellers and journalists of the period, were personages of no small importance in the public eye.

VIII

BOOKSELLERS OF THE REVOLUTION: PHILADELPHIA AND BOSTON

THE STATUS of the colonial bookseller, precarious in peace-time, became desperate during the Revolution. His market was broken, his property unsafe. One after another the chief cities fell into the hands of the British. There was still a Bradford in Philadelphia to bear his part in the fate of his country. Andrew Bradford, William's son, begot no children, but adopted a nephew, William Bradford the third, and bred him as a printer. Andrew's wife was fond of William and he was devoted to her. But she died when he was about nineteen, and Andrew later gave him a stepmother wicked enough to fit a fairy-tale. Let Isaiah Thomas set forth the facts: 'She had an adopted niece whom she was desirous that William Bradford, the adopted nephew of her husband, should marry when he became of age. William's affections being engaged by another object, the plan was frustrated; and in consequence she imbibed a settled prejudice against him, and did not attempt to conceal it. She treated him unkindly and finally he was obliged to leave the house of his foster-father. She prevailed on her husband to revoke the will which he had made in favor of William, and to make one in her own favor. It has been said that her conduct in general was such as rendered her husband very unhappy. William, when about twenty years of age, became the partner of Andrew; but the wife caused this partnership to be dissolved after it had continued one year.'

Soon after, William Bradford visited relatives in England. He came back with printing materials and a collection of books, set up a shop in Philadelphia, printed, sold books, and started a newspaper which survived into the next century. Andrew Bradford, it happened, died that year. The wicked stepmother kept his business going for a few years, but it does not appear that she could compete with young William; so that he had his revenge in Christian and legal fashion. He prospered at the Sign of the Bible in Black Horse Alley, and became a prominent citizen on the Whig side, serving as captain of militia. He married a daughter of the Thomas Budd who was arrested with the first William Bradford during the Quaker quarrel of 1690. And the later William proved himself a true chip off the block. He was among the first Philadelphians to oppose the Stamp Act in 1765. 'He took arms in an early stage of the Revolutionary War; and although he had reached the age at which the law exempts men from military service, he encountered the fatigues of a winter campaign, and did duty as a major of militia in the memorable battle of Trenton; he shared the honors of the day at Princeton, and returned colonel of the regiment of which he went out major. . . . A few days before the British troops took possession of Philadelphia, Bradford was entrusted by Governor Wharton with the command of the city and the superintendence of removing the stores. Having performed this duty, he left the city as the enemy was entering it, and repaired to Fort Mifflin, where he remained till that fortress was evacuated. From that time, Bradford remained at Trenton until the British army left Philadelphia, and reopened the printing house and coffee room; but the customs and manners of the citizens were changed, and he perceived that business had found new channels. He returned from the hazards of public service with a broken constitution and a shattered fortune.'* He died in 1791. His son Thomas, who was for some time his partner, rebuilt the business, and carried it on well into the nineteenth century.

So we follow the troubled record of the New York and Philadelphia booksellers through the Revolutionary period. The Bostonians fared much the same. There was the house of Edes and Gill, summarily wrecked by the coming of the British. Gill fell into the hands of the enemy. Edes continued his 'Boston Gazette' in Watertown, and became official printer for the provincial congress of Massachusetts. Both partners were ardent patriots. Both returned (though separately) to Boston and to printing after the British evacuation. But neither prospered greatly; their day was past. Gill retired in protest, 'seeing the press ready to be shackled with a *stamp act* fabricated

* Thomas, 'History of Printing.'

in his native state.' Edes outlived him to be forsaken by 'competence and ease,' and to die in poverty. Among Boston printers and booksellers on the Tory side was Ezekiel Russell. During some years before the Revolution he published a political paper called the 'Censor' which had Royalist support. He seems to have got into no serious difficulties with the patriotic element on this account, and to have been discreet, perhaps mute, during the war. Later he was active in Boston as a printer and a dealer in topical ballads and broadsides, distributed by street hawkers. Like so many of the colonial printers, he had a wife who was ready to take a hand at anything that concerned his business. Isaiah Thomas says she was 'indeed an helpmeet for him. She was a very industrious, active woman; she made herself acquainted with the printing business; and not only assisted her husband in the printing house, but she sometimes invoked her muse, and wrote ballads on recent tragical events, which being immediately printed, and set off with wooden cuts of coffins, etc. had frequently a considerable run.'

It is after his note on Ezekiel Russell that the learned and judicious Isaiah Thomas gives account of his own life and doings. He came of the best colonial stock. His father, however, seems to have been a waster, and 'having expended nearly all his patrimony, went abroad and died in Northcarolina; leaving his widow in narrow circumstances, with five dependent children.' She was of the strong breed, and not only supported her family by keeping a little shop in Boston but accumulated some property there. We get a hint of how this was possible from her son's laconic statement of his own case: 'When her son Isaiah was six years of age he was apprenticed by his mother to Zechariah Fowle' (the printer with the slender constitution whose brother once went to jail for him). His indentures bound the lad, from the age of six to his majority, 'to avoid drunkenness and the pursuit of carnal enjoyments and to serve his master truly.' The young Isaiah 'was soon employed to set types,' records the old Isaiah placidly; mounted on a high bench to make it possible. In his eighth year he set up the 'New England Primer,' for an edition that ran to 10,000 copies. Later he competed with Fleet's negro as a maker of 'cuts' printed from type-metal, for books and ballads issued by Fowle. Of a 'Book of Knowledge' for which he supplied the 'embellishments,' Thomas says, 'Bad as the cuts were executed, there was not at that time an artist who could have done much better. Some time before, and soon after, there were better engravers in Boston.' After a dozen years of partnership Thomas and Fowle had some disagreement, and separated.

Thomas wanted to go to England to learn the finer points of printing, but got no farther than Nova Scotia, where, in the employ of the only printer there, he soon proved himself worthy of a place among the independent and recalcitrant practitioners of his trade who so often appear in the foreground of our history. The Nova Scotia printer was lazy, and presently left his 'Halifax Gazette' in young Thom-

Heading of Isaiah Thomas's 'Massachusetts Spy', with the famous emblem of the Divided Snake originated by Franklin in 1754.

as's hands. The 'Gazette' took bold ground against the Stamp Act, and Thomas was officially reprimanded. The apprentice editor was more discreet thereafter; but when presently there was a popular demonstration against the Stamp Act, with the hanging of an effigy of the 'stampmaster' on the town gallows, Thomas was given credit for a part in the ceremonies. The sheriff called on him and threatened to jail him unless he gave the names of the chief actors in the demonstration. He refused, the sheriff tried to arrest him, but Thomas would not be taken without a warrant, and the matter went no further. From Halifax before long Isaiah set out as a traveling journeyman, and plied his trade in various places from New Hampshire to South Carolina. He came back to Boston in 1770, was formally released from his apprenticeship, entered some sort of partnership with his old master Zechariah Fowle, 'and began business by publishing "The Massachusetts Spy," a small newspaper printed three times a week.' He bought Fowle out after a few months. The 'Spy' became a semi-weekly and then a weekly. The war of the Revolution drew near, and the issue was joined. There was no question which side should be taken: Thomas openly announced that the 'Spy' would thenceforth 'be devoted to the Whig interest.' Tory pressure was put on him to support that side. He had taken over a debt of Fowle's to an officer of the Crown, and was in danger of losing his press and types. Under such conditions he might well have been cautious, but late in 1771 he printed a letter over the signature of 'Mucius Scaevola' that roused the authorities. Governor Hutchinson sent Thomas word that he was to appear before the Council. He replied 'that he was busily employed in his office, and could not wait upon his excellency and their honors.' The messenger returned with another demand for his attendance, and Thomas again refused. The question that then arose was the perennial question of authority and contempt. A lawyer advised Thomas to refuse to appear before the Council without a proper warrant. 'The council proceeded with caution, for the principle was at issue whether they possessed authority arbitrarily to summon whom they pleased before their board, to answer for their conduct.' The messenger appeared a third time with a verbal *order* for his attendance. Thomas demanded a written order. The authorities then tried to get at him by way of a libel suit, but a grand jury refused to indict him. Other attempts failed; but Thomas found himself in a hot place, with strong Tory feeling against him and open threats of violence being uttered by 'some of the British soldiery in town.' The pot of revolution was almost at the boil. A few days after Thomas had smuggled a press and types to the safety of Worcester, came the battle of Lexington (Thomas calls it 'the affair at Lexington'), in which he took part. He seems even to have been among the unsung Reveres and Daweses of the famous alarm: 'On the night of April 18, 1775, it was discovered that a considerable number of British troops were embarking in boats on the river near the common, with the manifest design to destroy the stores collected by the provincials at Concord, eighteen miles from Boston; and he was concerned, with others, in giving the alarm. At daybreak the next morning he crossed over to Charlestown, went to Lexington, and joined the provincial militia in opposing the King's troops. On the 20th, he went to Worcester, opened a printing house, and soon after recommenced the publication of his newspaper.'*

In Worcester he remained, to serve for some time as official printer for Congress. At the end of the war he opened a bookstore in Worcester, and later established branches, both for printing and bookselling, in Boston, Walpole, N. H., Brookfield, Mass., Albany, and Baltimore. It was a time, as his 'History' shows, when many of the old printers were failing. Thomas was among the few who were industrious and adroit enough to meet the changed conditions brought about by the Revolution. At one time sixteen presses were at work for him and his various partners, in different places. They did a great business in Bibles and geographies, and published many lay books. Thomas printed and issued the 'Massachusetts Magazine' in Boston for five years. In 1802 he resigned control of the business to his son Isaiah Thomas Jr., under whose imprint the 'History of Printing' was issued in 1810.

On the title-page of that classic work the author appears as 'Isaiah Thomas, Printer,' and at seventy-eight he said, 'Could I live my life over again and

* Thomas, 'History of Printing.'

choose my employment, it would be that of a printer.' He is recognized as one of the master-printers of his time: Franklin went so far as to call him 'the Baskerville of America.' He was also one of the most notable publishers and booksellers, as well as an invaluable historian of matters that but for him would have been forgotten. As a collector of Americana he was among the earliest and greatest. He more than any American up to his time realized the importance of preserving national publications and records. He founded the American Antiquarian Society, and gave it 3,000 volumes as nucleus for a library. He paid for the first building occupied by the Society, and his gifts to it, first and last, came to more than $50,000. When he died Governor Lincoln 'pronounced a eulogy,' in which he said: 'With a strong and vigorous mind and cultivated intellect, energy, enterprise and industry in early life gave him wealth, and possessed of this he lived in courtly style and with beneficent liberality. He was the first in town to keep a carriage, and had his colored coachman in livery. . . . His attention to appearance and dress was singularly precise and studied.' In later life he was prominent in all State and local movements for the public good. He belonged to many learned societies and had several degrees. A man who did credit to his trade and to his race, and whose name should not be forgotten.

IX

THE POST-REVOLUTIONARY PERIOD

Though Thomas's 'History of Printing' was published in 1810, it has little to say of printing and bookselling after the Revolution, and nothing of those who began work after the war. Even Matthew Carey is not mentioned. But it was with Carey and one or two others, notably Charles Wiley and the Harpers, that modern American bookselling and publishing actually began. Thomas was of an older generation, and for all his intelligence seems hardly to have been aware of the new airs that were beginning to blow through a young land. The war had banished, with the tens of thousands of Tory exiles, much of our best blood and our best culture. Raw problems of political practice and material development were pressing on all sides. Pamphleteering went on vigorously, satire flourished, the newspaper began to be something more than a belated bulletin of every-day events. It was not the hour for creative writing. Most books printed here were still of British source, the old standbys mainly, Young's 'Night Thoughts' and Baxter's 'Saints' Rest,' Milton, Sterne, Thomson, Pope, Defoe. Our exultation in the new political independence did not overcome a sort of inferiority complex in matters intellectual and aesthetic. Yet there were signs of the awakening of a nationalist impulse in letters, and here and there a plea for buying American books as such. In 1786 the president of Harvard recommended Nicholas Pike's 'Complete System of Arithmetic,' on the ground that it was 'wholly American in work and execution,' and would keep American money in this country. Before the end of the century Noah Webster had begun to work for American independence in matters of diction, pronunciation, and spelling, and Jedediah Morse had made a name in Europe as an American geographer—and a good living here.

The uncertain status of publishing in the eighteenth century is illustrated by a passage in Isaiah Thomas about the well-known Ames 'Almanack': 'John Draper and his predecessor Bartholomew Green had always purchased the copy of that Almanack, and printed it on their own account; but they had supplied the booksellers in sheets, by the hundred, the thousand, or any quantity wanted. About the year 1759 this Almanack was enlarged from sixteen pages on a foolscap sheet to three and a half sheets. Draper formed a connexion with Green and Russell, and T. and J. Fleet, in its publication. A half-sheet was printed at each of their printing houses; and they were not disposed to supply booksellers as formerly. The booksellers, immediately on the publication of the Almanack, had it reprinted; and soon after a number of them set up a printing house for themselves; and they engaged Daniel Kneeland,

and John his brother, to conduct it for them.' Here you have a printer acting as publisher, buying the copy and selling his product direct to the booksellers. When he stops selling to them, they openly pirate the product, and proceed to do their own printing and publishing.

Soon after the Revolution a beginning was made toward regulating or regularizing the relations of author, publisher, and public. The Act of 1790 made an American author proprietor of his work for fourteen years only. A letter to Matthew Carey by Noah Webster shows a method of distribution made necessary by difficulties of transportation, and possible by friendly co-operation among booksellers. Webster sold the rights in his 'Grammatical Institute' to seven proprietors, each of whom was supposed to confine himself to his own territory. There was no law against a bookseller's marketing his wares where he chose, but a gentlemen's agreement was enough. 'The proprietors have no difference with each other and no clashing; they are restrained by agreement as well as by the inconvenience of sending their books abroad.' Did the lexicographer smile to himself as he wrote this? A moment later he repeated that the proprietors were kept from poaching on each other's preserves 'only by their honor and convenience.' They had also agreed not to undersell each other. It all sounds Utopian, auguring well indeed for harmonious co-operation among the citizens of the new republic. Alas! the secret of it lay largely in the item of convenience, and in lack of acute provocation.

Popular though Webster's learned spellers and grammars were, they were not the kind of spoils men fight over. The era of huge popular favorites or 'best-sellers' was yet to come.

Already, to be sure, there were portents. In 1786 America produced a romantic yarn by one James Buckland, called: 'An Account of the Discovery of a Hermit, Who lived about 200 Years in a Cave at the Foot of a Hill, 73 Days' Journey Westward of the Great Alleghany Mountains.' It was a crude thriller, by modern standards, but it had an extraordinary circulation; was printed that year in at least five towns. Not long afterward, the novels of Brockden Brown gained some hearing on account of his American settings and his realism of detail. But his master for mood and type was an English contemporary, William Godwin. Brown may be called our first professional author. A Philadelphia Quaker by birth, at twenty-seven he published his first romance, 'Wieland,' and wrote four others in the next five years. He edited two magazines, wrote many pamphlets on politics and the rights of women, and died fashionably of 'consumption,' still short of forty.

The rill of pure letters flowed thin, those years. There were Philip Freneau and his fellow-satirists, John Trumbull, Joel Barlow, Timothy Dwight, and Francis Hopkinson. Their work was effective and often brilliant, but it followed old models. There was more meaning for the future in Brockden Brown's attempts in the new field of prose fiction. It was a field still under suspicion in most of the young

States, though Hugh Gaine the New Yorker had been bold enough to reprint English plays and novels as early as the 1760's. They were frowned on till much later in New England—in Philadelphia, for that matter, since in 1800 a printer anxiously queries of Matthew Carey whether he 'can think of publishing a novel?' Still, Evans lists as published in America between 1786 and 1789, 38 plays, 43 novels, and 104 children's books. Many of these last, no doubt, like Matthew Carey's edition of 'Goody Twoshoes,' were reprints from Newbery's English series of 'juveniles.' Our output was still largely imitative. Massachusetts had been especially hard hit by the exile of her cultivated Tories. Emerson said that Massachusetts produced 'not a book, a speech, a conversation or a thought, between 1790 and 1820.' The Hartford Wits, Dwight, Barlow, and Trumbull, were content to echo the jig-metre of 'Hudibras' or the prim couplets of Pope. Our prose writers followed Addison or Johnson; our novelists whispered hollowly in the corridors of Udolpho and Otranto. It was not till the second decade of the nineteenth century that, with Irving and Cooper and Bryant and Halleck, our writers began to express the national character and scene by way of dealing with American materials.

Meanwhile a great publisher had emerged in Matthew Carey of Philadelphia. He was a pioneer in the post-Revolutionary movement toward literary independence. As a publisher of American books and founder of the first successful American magazine, he left a permanent mark on the national life. He was born in Dublin in 1760, had good elementary schooling, and at fifteen chose to be apprenticed to a bookseller. His father did not approve, and suggested twenty other callings as preferable. But the boy knew what he wanted. He read avidly, and was interested in public affairs. At seventeen he wrote an article against dueling, at nineteen he published a pamphlet calling on the Catholics of Ireland to rebel against a Penal Code deliberately aimed at them. The authorities resented this, a reward was offered for his arrest. He escaped to France and Passy. There Franklin engaged him to reprint despatches from America. He was, you would think, a lad after Franklin's heart, but it was Lafayette who took a strong fancy to him. If Carey had Franklin's industry, he had Lafayette's impulsive and generous nature. Later he worked with the great French printer Didot. After a year or so he found it safe to come back to Ireland. His first offence had blown over. But almost at once he was headed for more hot water. He began the publication of a 'Volunteer's Journal,' defending Irish rights against England. His countrymen hailed it with joy, but he was promptly arrested and jailed in Newgate. His release by political influence left him under the menace of a prosecution for libeling the Premier. He decided to turn to a new and freer world, and landed at Philadelphia in 1784 'with only a few guineas in his pocket.' Lafayette, then visiting at Mount Vernon, heard of Carey's arrival and sent him $400, with which he proceeded to set up a daily newspaper, the 'Pennsylvania Herald.' The feature that brought it success was his full reporting from memory of the debates of the State Assembly.

Philadelphia was then our unchallenged metropolis, much larger than New York, twice as large as Boston. Carey was Irish and born for trouble; his instinct had carried him to the spot where most trouble could be found. In theory he was more firebrand than fire-eater. But his boyish essay against dueling could be forgotten at a pinch. Within a year he had fought a duel with a Philadelphian and been properly winged. His opponent was a Colonel Oswald, who ran the rival (Federalist) newspaper, the 'Independent Gazetteer.' Oswald had tried to block Carey from the start. The two editors got to swapping personalities, and this meant highly colored language in those days. Among other things, Carey wrote and printed a satirical poem at Oswald's expense, 'The Scurriliad.' Oswald challenged, they met, and Carey went to bed for sixteen months with a bullet in his thigh. Oswald and he became friends later. During his invalidism the 'Herald' lapsed, but, not long after, Carey started a monthly, the 'Columbian Magazine,' short-lived like most of its kind, a tame assortment of materials chiefly filched from British sources. But he saw his way to something better, and almost at once produced the 'American Museum,' which survived for several years. It not only reprinted a large body of the best writing of the time, British and American, but also published a good deal of original matter by the cream of our native writers,

Franklin, Freneau, Trumbull, Hopkinson, and Noah Webster.

Moreover, like Isaiah Thomas, Carey had a strong sense of the importance of preserving contemporary records and documents, and published much of this material in the 'Museum.' The magazine achieved some circulation both here and abroad. It was highly praised by Washington, who hailed its superiority to earlier magazines and the service it was doing for American culture. But it was a costly product, and the low price at which it had to be sold precluded any profit. Carey discontinued it, in 1792, without obvious chagrin. There were other fish in his sea. Just then he was (as he wrote a brother in Dublin) 'entering pretty largely into the printing and bookselling business.' Already he had published a number of books 'on his own account.' He enclosed a list which shows how large a range he proposed to cover, and how far (like all other booksellers of the time) he was from the specialization that was to rule the trade half a century later. A history of New York, 'Necker on Religion,' 'Beauties of Poetry,' 'Beatty's Morals,' 'Ladies' Library,' 'Garden of the Soul,' 'Douay Bible,' Trumbull's 'McFingal,' and several minor works. He is, he says, about to issue Blair's 'Lectures,' and has written to London, Dublin, and Glasgow 'for a supply of foreign books, without which I cannot have a proper assortment.'

Carey prospered as publisher and bookseller. He had convictions, enterprise, and the dreadful virtue of industry so worshiped in that age. 'For twenty-five years,' says Thomas, 'he was present every morning when the shutters of his store were taken down for the day.' Franklin had set the precedent for this kind of thing in Philadelphia, by both precept and practice. In the early days of his publishing, Carey was much 'on the road,' getting subscriptions and collecting accounts; selling books in parcels, too, among the village merchants. A letter of 1789 reads: 'In three weeks of last month I rode 650 miles, on a horse that cost me only 22 dollars. I made slight preparation for the journey, and the total expense of the 650 miles was not over £8.' But it was not many years before other men were doing the traveling for him. Mason Locke Weems, 'Parson Weems,' had some sort of business dealings with Carey as early as 1790, and a few years later was spending much of his time on the road as Carey's agent.

Parson Weems is so picturesque a figure in the annals of American bookselling, and for that matter in the history of his time, that his story is worth a little space in our record. Clergyman, man of the world, author, publisher, humorist, hawker of books, he passed through life with gusto, with honor, and with profit. Born in America, he went abroad at thirteen, and studied medicine three years in London and Edinburgh. He was surgeon aboard a British man-of-war till the Revolution: he came home in 1776. Oddly enough, it is not known where he was or what he did during the early years of the war. In 1782, before peace was declared, he determined to take orders in the Church of England, the church of our Southern aristocracy. There was no American bishop to ordain him here, and he could not be frocked in England without taking the oath of allegiance to the Crown. Two years later Parliament passed an Act dispensing with the oath for persons who were to serve in the colonies. Weems was ordained that year, and came home to be rector of a Maryland parish for five years. He also ran a school for girls, at that time, and was proud later on of having been an occasional incumbent of Pohick, George Washington's church.

He was a mellow divine after the eighteenth century British pattern, worlds away from the puritan austerity of the New England ministers. The convivial habits of the Maryland gentry did not offend him. He thought it well to be 'cheerful in his mien that he might win men to religion.' He was a lover of his kind, made pets of children and negroes. He was of picaresque temper, 'born for the road,' says his biographer.* There is a tradition that he carried a fiddle in his book van, and fiddled for dancing, on occasion. It is certain that by about 1792 he had given up the ministry and become a traveling vendor, at first of religious and moral works but later, as Carey's agent, of all sorts of books issued or imported by that eminent publisher. He also sold great numbers of books and pamphlets written by himself and published at his own risk. Sometimes he called at private houses, like a modern book agent, to solicit

* Wroth, 'Parson Weems.'

subscriptions or dispose of books from his van. Sometimes he opened his wares in taverns; and many books were sold in lots to local merchants at reduced prices. He hired subagents, giving them a copy for every six subscriptions placed, or offering a free copy with every four paid for on the nail. 'Counting me down 256 Dol (32 sets),' he writes Carey, of one such deal, 'he gladly took up 40 sets.' Carey and Weems sometimes fell out, but their relations were usually cordial and often jocose. Carey posts letters to 'Mason L. Weems, Esq., Parson, Traveling Bookseller, &c., &c.' Weems writes his reports in a bubbling and exuberant style that would make a modern employer stare and gasp. The published correspondence of these two, ranging over thirty years, is a fascinating study of the writers, as well as a varied commentary on bookselling in America from 1795 to 1825.*

For all his roving tastes, Weems was by no means absent-minded about practical matters, and we find him periodically trying to get just a little more commission out of his employer. In 1796 he writes: 'I hope that at this time of day I hardly need assure you that I had much rather subscriptioneer and vend books for you than for any other man whatever. But yet I well know that you are, like Brutus, an honorable man, and would not exact a bond of barren services from anyone, and least of all from a most devoted friend. Now that your allowance to me (in the store settling business, I mean) is rather of the lean and bobtailed kind, may, I would hope, be easily

* Skeel, 'Mason Locke Weems: His Works and Ways.'

demonstrated to your entire satisfaction. You allow me 5 per cent for books sold by commission. Well, I'll *suppose* that I am going down to Richmond to place in proper hands a box of books. . . . This box, by a second supposition, is worth 300 Dol. The sum total of my profits on the box wholly sold is 15 Dol.

> Stage hire from Dumfries to Richmond, 5 Dol.
>   Do back again,   5 Dol.
> Expenses on road for 3 days & 4 nights, 5 Dol.
>   15 Dol.

Here you see that without the help of drams for drivers, half bits for poor Negro waiters, or any of those countless petty larceny robberies to which flesh and blood on the highways is heir, I have fairly got clear of all my five percent for a trunk containing 300 Dollars. Thus after rolling & jolting, tumbling and tossing through a journey of 200 miles, rous'd from sweet sleep at one o'clock in the morning, coop'd up in a common stage for almost three days and nights together, my head aching from loss of rest, my ears startl'd with female screams or masculine imprecations and whole senses stun'd with rattling wheels, cracking whips, rushing water & clouds of dust I at length get home, not to exult like Buonaparte over his ducats and florins, but to mourn with old Naomi: "Woe's me, for I went out full, but the Lord hath brought me back empty." '

The upshot is, Naomi wants 10 per cent: 'A tythe

was always assign'd to the family of Levi, and that by some of them was look'd on as a rather touch and go sort of allowance,' but Weems means to be satisfied with it. Five years later he is complaining of a 25 per cent commission and asking 33 1/3. But the earlier 5 per cent seems to have been on sales of books in lots to dealers, while the larger commission was probably for single subscriptions. Books were costly then, and it is amazing how many of them were sold to a people struggling with the after-effects of war. Weems now and then complains of Carey's prices. People think them too dear. 'For God's sake,' he cries, with a twinkle in his reverend eye, 'For God's sake sell Divinity cheap!' Divinity, for some time, was an important part of his wares. He sold also great numbers of Goldsmith's 'Animated Nature,' and of his own 'Life of Washington,' published by Carey. This work ran through fifty editions or more and, among other books by Weems, was widely read till the middle of the nineteenth century.

Weems was always full of ideas, quite willing to teach Carey his business, and bubbling over with semi-humorous protestations. The stock Carey sends him is too small, or not varied enough. Surely the general in the field should know what ammunition he needs: 'I am he who leads this squadron to the charge, and therefore can best tell whether it [the current consignment] be indeed prepared to meet every assailant.' Conditions he finds always annoying, often intolerable. In 1803 he writes that he is about to quit the field, after eight years, 'without a shilling.'

Fifteen years later he is of the same mind. I find a letter of that time to Carey cited without the author's name: surely it bears all the Weems earmarks: 'You may in mind assimilate my business to water running down hill, but let me tell you it would be more just if you compared it to a shad climbing a pine tree.' But these two understood and deserved each other. Their connection persisted till Weems's death in 1825.

Forgotten for a time, Weems bids fair to be remembered not merely as the fabricator of the hatchet and cherry-tree fable, but as an engaging and notable personality. Dr. Wroth's delightful monograph, 'Parson Weems,' has been unceremoniously plumped up into popular form by another hand, and a third biography is in sight.

Carey's fame still rests, and may well rest, upon the study by Professor Bradsher.* He was easily leader among the post-Revolutionary publishers south of New England. Isaiah Thomas, with headquarters at Worcester and branches elsewhere, was firm in his saddle, but distance and difficulty of transportation prevented active rivalry with the Philadelphian. Carey was the younger and more venturesome of the two. Thomas, patriotic though he was, always based his publication largely on reprints. Importation had been abruptly cut off by the war. In 1782 Robert Aiken of Philadelphia issued the first English Bible printed in America. There was a great increase

* Bradsher, 'Mathew Carey.'

The Post-Revolutionary Period 137

in American editions of standard English works, like Blackstone, Dr. Johnson, and Adam Smith. Carey had fine dreams of co-operation among members of the trade. In 1802 he issued a call for all American printers and booksellers to assemble for the purpose of forming an association on the lines of the British Stationers' Company. Carey drew up a constitution. The first meeting was held in New York, with the veteran Hugh Gaine as president. The new association was called 'The American Company of Booksellers.' Rather strangely, the word stationer seems not to have been used even among early colonial booksellers. The purpose of the society was to promote co-operation, largely through the exchange of books and the regulation of territories. The Company was a success for a few years, but then, as usually happens, unscrupulous competition wrecked the fine theory of mutual justice: 'The less important and more remote publishers produced large editions of popular works on cheap paper, and with worn and broken type, with which by means of the exchange they flooded the country. Naturally the more prominent publishers, the leaders in the company, who had in many cases good editions of these books on hand, soon withdrew, and the movement collapsed.'*

* Bradsher, 'Mathew Carey.'

X

THE TURN OF THE CENTURY

At the turn of the century and for some time thereafter the cost of manufacturing books remained large and their prices high. The stereotyping method had been invented long before, but America was slow to adopt it, and England slower. G. H. Putnam says its use was not common in England even in the 1850's. After an edition was set up and printed, the type was distributed, and no second impression could be made. Matthew Carey kept his quarto Bible in type for many years. Some of the chases were not touched till 1844, when they were broken up to use the brevier type of the notes for a cheap edition of Rory O'More—a fate which might have amused merry Parson Weems more than his friend Carey. Few printers could afford to tie up their types in that fashion. The cost of illustration ('embellishment' was still the word) was almost prohibitive till lithography came in, about 1820. Paper and ink were of poor quality and typography crude; though the Booksellers' Company did some service by offering prizes for the best samples of ink, paper, and printing. American first editions even of the 1830's are the despair of collectors who crave 'condition,' on account of the almost invariable 'foxing'

From Lanier's 'A Century of Banking in New York'
Courtesy of Doubleday, Doran & Company.

BROADWAY AND WALL STREET ABOUT 1820. THE SECOND BUILDING ON THE RIGHT WAS CHARLES WILEY'S BOOK STORE.

The Turn of the Century 139

due to the use of rags from which needles and other ironware had not been removed before pulping.

For some years after the Revolution, as we have seen, the book trade had been without any keen spur of competition to endanger the relations of the traders. Markets were localized; the publishers all issued about the same kind of books. Then, rather suddenly, a new actor entered the stage of bookmaking—the novel. Toward the end of the century the sensational British romances headed by 'The Mysteries of Udolpho' and 'Charlotte Temple' had roused a new taste for light reading on both sides of the water. But you cannot play variations forever on a jews-harp. By 1810 the conventionalized mystery and horror of that school had gone stale. Jane Austen mocked it in 'Northanger Abbey,' and took her part in the establishing of a new taste for a fiction builded, whether romantically or not, on certain primary elements of common experience and common sense. By 1811 a Pittsburgh bookseller could write that novels were 'all the rage' there. Means of communication were improving. Roads were better. The physical item of 'convenience' lost its weight as a regulator of book distribution. The idea (or the reality) of the 'best seller' took hold of the book trade. Every publisher became eager to get large profits out of the few popular books instead of small profits from an extended general list. Byron and Scott became the special booty to be fought for; and it was not long before all friendly scruples were cast aside, and

American bookselling became frankly a process of dog eat dog. As foreign work had no protection here, the publisher who could get hold of the proof-sheets or the earliest printed copies of the latest canto of 'Don Juan' or the latest 'Waverley Novel,' had a certain advantage, like the first homesteader over the line in a land-rush. But he couldn't stake his claim; he could only get in a day's work before the pack was all about him, crowding him away from his place.

Until the novel usurped the scene, then, Matthew Carey had been content to do a general business. When the rush for Scott and Byron (that versifying novelist) began, he was able to get the inside track for awhile. He imported early sheets by arrangement with Constable. For safety, they would be shipped in different packets, but even then, says Bradsher, 'the uncertainties of the voyage always rendered it doubtful whether some rival might not obtain an ordinary copy almost, if not quite as soon. When the sheets were received, therefore, relays of compositors worked over them night and day, and as soon as the binder finished his work a stage-coach would be chartered to carry to New York the supplies required for that city. This was regarded at that time as a wonderful exhibition of enterprise, and Mr. William A. Blanchard, who entered Mr. Carey's service as a boy, in 1812, used to relate how he would be sent off in charge of a stage-load of a "Waverley," and travel perched upon the bundles of books, night and day, to be ferried across the North River and deliver his packages to the various booksellers of New York—a service not without hardship and even risk, in inclement seasons.'*

Certain letters between the Careys and John Miller, their London agent, show how the battle was carried on. For £25 a volume Miller buys for Carey a first chance at publishing 'Peveril of the Peak' in America; he is to have 'the last sheets, at least 14 days before they publish in Edinburgh, which will secure you from all danger of disappointment.' Carey printed the sheets as fast as they were received, so that he was in a position to 'have it all out within 24 hours from the time the last part is received. Still, if a complete copy arrived in New York with ours, they could print it in the time it requires our copy to come here and go back. . . . The only advantage we derive from the purchase is the sale of three or four days until another Edit. can be published in New York, Boston, and here.' The following year the Careys write to Miller, 'We have received "Quentin Durward" most handsomely and have the Game completely in our hands this time. In 28 hours after receiving it, we had 1500 copies sent off or ready to go, and the whole Edition is now nearly distributed. In two days we shall publish it here and in New York, and the Pirates may print it as soon as they please. The opposition Edition will be out in about 48 hours after they have one of our copies but we shall have complete and entire posses-

* Bradsher, 'Mathew Carey.'

sion of every market in the country for a short time.'

It was a lively game. When 'The Monastery,' 'The Abbot,' and 'Ivanhoe' all came out in the same year, 1820, the American book trade must have felt much like the chameleon on the piece of plaid. By then the amenities had been laid aside. Complaints and recriminations flew back and forth among the contenders, but there were no rules to break, and the gentlemen's agreement had gone by the board. The emergence of a large reading public for the novel, like a gold-strike, had temporarily suspended a code of manners and honor that belonged to normal and civilized times. There are almost incredible anecdotes of the measures taken to get the top cream of the market. Thomas McElrath, of McElrath and Bangs, New York makers and sellers of schoolbooks and religious books, recalled an experience of his boyhood in the office of Carey and Lea in Philadelphia. He was, he said, 'the first person in the United States who read the 11th, 12th, and 13th cantos of Lord Byron's "Don Juan." Carey & Lea received an advance copy which, before cutting the leaves, was sent to the then famous printing office of William Brown in Philadelphia, where it was immediately given out to thirty or forty compositors, and within thirty-six hours an American edition was on sale at the bookstores.' Young McElrath read the proofs. This was in 1823. A little later the competition became especially keen between the Careys and the Harpers. J. C. Derby has

The Turn of the Century 143

a tale to tell of the ruthless warfare they waged for British booty:

'In 1836 Carey & Hart had received an advance copy of Bulwer's "Rienzi" from the English publisher, for which they paid a liberal sum. The Harpers had also received an advance copy by the same packet, there being no steamers in those days; then came the rivalry to see who would first supply the market with early copies. Mr. Hart says that on the day it was received, they distributed the sheets of this advance copy among twelve different printers, in order to produce the book before the Harpers put theirs on the market; and by nine o'clock the next morning the sheets of the whole edition were delivered to the binders, who had the cases already made in shape for binding. That same afternoon, 500 complete copies were forwarded to New York booksellers by the mail stage, the only conveyance by which they could reach New York by daylight the following morning, and this could only be accomplished by hiring all the passenger seats. Mr. Hart was the only passenger of the stage that morning, the remaining space in the coach being taken up with Bulwer's "Rienzi." The volume was for sale in all the New York bookstores one day earlier than Harper's edition of the same work.'*

Physically the Harpers had the advantage, as most of the books from England passed through New York. Her position as a seaport had much to do with the New Yorkers' later supremacy over Phila-

* Derby, 'Fifty Years.'

delphians in the book and other markets. They often triumphed over the Careys, and were especially pleased to bag Moore's 'Life of Byron,' an immensely popular tidbit. Small wonder that these reprints were greatly inferior in make-up and typography to the English originals. There is painful contrast between the fair page of the Constable 'Waverleys' and the huddled look of the editions rushed out by the Careys and others. The English three-decker was compressed here into two volumes; and this was the rule thereafter. Some of the native American work was much better printed. The early Irvings were respectable examples of bookmaking, and the Coopers issued by Charles Wiley were of far more presentable typography than the later novels that appeared under the Carey imprint. But Wiley got a better price, for reasons that will presently appear.

These cut-throat conditions of the early nineteenth century book trade had one notable effect. They forced many publishers to specialize in fields where competition was not so general and returns were more stable. Many firms withdrew altogether from the publication of belles-lettres to the field of the schoolbook, the religious or medical book, or the manual of technical or scientific content. But among the few powerful caterers for popular entertainment the battle went on for many years, with unhappy results, as we shall see, for both foreign and native authors. Through the first two decades of the century American publishing was still uncentral-

The Turn of the Century 145

ized. A few firms stood out from the ruck, Thomas in New England, Carey in Philadelphia, the Harpers in New York. But there were many smaller men in these cities who had a finger in the pie, and most of the printers in the smaller towns were also, soon or late, editors, booksellers, and publishers. If you look over any miscellaneous assortment of books printed here during the generation following the Revolution you will find such imprints as Reading, Lancaster, and Germantown in Pennsylvania, Portsmouth in New Hampshire, Hartford and New Haven in Connecticut, Newport and Providence in Rhode Island, Charleston in South Carolina, Lexington in Kentucky, and Albany in New York.

In 1837 Carey & Co. issued the 'Pickwick Papers' in parts and, addressing 'Mr. Saml. Dickens' (perhaps confounding his author with Mr. Weller), offered a draft for '£25 at 4 mos. which we beg you will accept not as a compensation, but as a memento of the fact that unsolicited a bookseller has sent an author, if not money, at least a fair representative of it. The amt. is small, and you can well understand why it is not more when we state that we shall sell the whole 12 pts., done up in 3 vols to the trade for about five shillings net: After paying the cost of making, this does not leave much for the Bookseller or Author.' Dickens, just emerging from obscurity with the sudden popularity of 'Pickwick' in England, recognizes the offer as a gracious gesture, but rather oddly declines it: 'I should not feel, under the circumstances, quite at ease in drawing upon you for the amount you so liberally request me to consider you my debtors in, but I shall have very great pleasure in receiving from you an American copy of the work, which coupled with your very handsome letter, I shall consider a sufficient acknowledgment of the American sale.' Within five years Dickens had come to take a very different attitude, realizing how vast were the sales of his work in America, and how impossible any real share of the profits for the author. The failure of his efforts for an international copyright law during his visit to America in 1842 ended in disgust and resentment which are expressed in a letter to Lea and Blanchard after his return. He washes his hands of any future American republications of his work. The American people shall 'have the full pride, honor, glory and profit of it'; he will be 'no party to its invasion,' and will 'have nothing blown to him by a side wind, which the dishonest breath of the popular legislature withheld. I hope,' he concludes, 'that the more you see of this plunder and the dirty hands into which it goes, the more you will feel and advocate the necessity of change.' His fear that 'there was no reasonable hope of such a change for many years' was justified in the event; it was almost an even half-century later that the first copyright agreement between England and America was attained.

With the public so fatally seduced by its new charmer the novel, the market for more solid literary fare steadily declined. The classics were neglected, English poetry was in little demand, and

American poetry was totally ignored. In 1818 Carey wrote Freneau, veteran and survivor of our first group of native poets, that the last edition of his poems, 1,000 copies, was nearly sold out—after nine years: 'The demand here has ceased.' Three years later the first running of our clearest stream of poetry, Bryant's 'Poems' of 1821, was issued in an edition of 650 copies. Two hundred and seventy of them were disposed of in five years. Only Cooper among American writers, and he only in the character of romantic novelist, could hold his own against the current of imported and cheaply reprinted fiction. Between the 1820's and the 1840's, though a true American literature was then emerging, matters went from bad to worse for the American writer and for all but a few American publishers, so far as the publication of original imaginative writing was concerned. In 1840 and 1841 Cooper succeeded in 'coming back' with two more 'Leatherstocking Tales': but that was the end for him as a money-making author. In 1841 the Careys declined to publish a new collection of tales by Poe. His 'Tales of the Grotesque and Arabesque' (1840) had been of 750 copies. The publisher writes that it is not yet sold, 'and up to this time it has not returned to us the expense of its publication.' Alas, poor Yorick! A copy of those tales is now worth three or four hundred dollars. In the same year the Careys complain to William Gilmore Simms that his latest book 'Confession' is a total failure: 'We do not see much hope in the future for the American writer of light literature—as a matter of profit it might be abandoned. The channel seems to be glutted with periodical literature, particularly the mammoth weeklies—besides which we go into market for $1.50 a copy against English reprints at 90c.'

And there we have it. The cheap reprints of unprotected English fiction made the American product unsalable on any terms of profit for publisher or author. Some of Cooper's novels were issued in paper at twenty-five cents a volume. This, says Professor Bradsher, had the effect of developing the American magazine and the American short story. But England continued to furnish us with our favorite fiction, unlimited in quantity and dirt cheap: Scott, Bulwer, Marryatt, Disraeli, Thackeray, and above all Dickens, who made the fortunes of several American publishers and bitterly refused to dicker with them for the pennies they offered.

For nearly three decades of the new century Carey continued to dominate the field. By 1820 he had built up a world-wide trade, with exchanges or agents in various parts of Europe and South America. In 1817 a son, Henry C. Carey, was taken into the firm, and a little later a son-in-law, Isaac Lea. Matthew Carey retired in 1824, but remained an adviser and backer of 'Carey & Lea.' Further mutations of the firm's title are puzzling to readers who come in contact with them in following the story of publishing for the next fifty years. Soon after Matthew left it, a younger son entered the firm and for a time the name was Carey, Lea & Carey. In 1829 the business was divided, the latest partner, Edward L. Carey, taking over the retail trade in partnership with Abraham Hart. Carey & Hart later became Carey, Baird & Co. Carey & Lea continued expanding as publishers, though now the Harpers and the Appletons had begun to press them from the north. In 1833 the firm became Carey, Lea & Blanchard, then Lea & Blanchard, Blanchard & Lea, Henry C. Lea, Henry C. Lea's Son & Co.: the 'son,' Charles M. Lea, was fourth in descent from Matthew Carey. In 1885, the firm became Lea Brothers & Co. The house kept always to a high standard both in the quality of its output and in its business ethics, with an old-fashioned sense of 'moral responsibility' that one looks back to with a smile and a sigh. There are times when the reader equipped with rudimentary self-respect must feel that if those old ideas of decency were cant and repression, they were pleasanter to live with than the cant and expression of our day.

Matthew Carey was one of the leading citizens of his time and place. When the dreaded yellow fever took possession of Philadelphia in 1793 he belonged to the committee of citizens, including leaders like Stephen Girard, who stayed in the city and kept things under control. His 'Short Account' of the episode ran through a dozen editions, and may almost stand with Defoe's 'Journal of the Plague Year' in London. Brockden Brown gave a more highly colored picture of that ghastly year in Philadelphia, in 'Arthur Mervyn.' In 1810 Carey took an important part in the agitation for the rechartering of the Bank of the United States, and did some especially effective pamphleteering for the cause. He did a good deal of later writing on banking. Indeed he was the founder of a new school of political economy: almost a dynasty, since his son Henry C. Carey and his grandson Henry Carey Baird followed him as theorists and writers in that field. He became interested in the subject by way of his efforts to improve the conditions of American industry during the War of 1812. His 'Olive Branch: or Faults on Both Sides' (1814) had great effect. It was written to bring together quarreling factions and to unite them against England. His study of existing conditions led to the study of books. He fell foul of Adam Smith, the accepted authority of the time, became an early apostle of the protective tariff, and with little support continued to issue, year after year, his arguments in favor of that method. His early books on banking matters were followed by a series published in the 1820's: 'Essays on Political Economy' (1822), 'An Appeal to Common Sense' (1823), 'The Crisis' (1823), 'The Political Economist' (1824), 'Prospects on and Beyond the Rubicon' (1830), and 'An Appeal to the Wealthy of the Land' (1836). These were controversial pamphlets centring in the advocacy of the protective system, and of great influence in their day. Henry C. Carey's first book, 'An Essay on the Rate of Wages,' appeared a year before Matthew's last. H. C. Carey in the course of the next forty years gained an international reputation by various works on political economy. He began as a free trader, but seems to have become an independent convert to his father's faith. He developed original theories opposed to those generally held by British economists. His nephew Henry Carey Baird was a person of equally decided views. He did not hesitate to come out flatly against an international copyright law on theoretical grounds, at a time when some other New York publishers were assenting to the principle and secretly opposing the practice.

But Matthew Carey is remembered as the great man of the tribe. Poe, who had been handled shabbily by the younger Careys, paid tribute to his strength and honesty; and his biographer, on good evidence, holds him up as 'one of the greatest publishers, all things considered in their true historical perspective, yet produced by this country.'

XI

NEW YORK ARRIVES

PHILADELPHIA, we have seen, was still in the lead as a publishing centre when the nineteenth century came in. Forces were stirring that would change this. But New Yorkers were still devoted to business and pleasure, not to culture. They lived in the counting-house by day, and by night tasted the gaieties of the little cosmopolitan town: for so it was already. Manhattan had an atmosphere quite different from the primness of Philadelphia or the gravity of Boston. Among the upper class came a belated flowering of eighteenth century gallantry. The mood of the rising generation was a blend of sentiment and mockery. In 1807 the 'Salmagundi' papers of Irving and Paulding laughed at town types and follies very much in the fashion of the 'Tatler' a century earlier and the 'New Yorker' a century later. The circumstances of its publication are interesting as they show the hit-or-miss conditions of publishing at the time. Its authors expressly disclaimed any idea of profit, for their publisher David Longworth as well as for themselves. According to Pierre Irving this Longworth, whom they called 'Dusky Davie,' suggested that they take out a copyright 'but they did not think it worth while, and he thereupon took it out himself.'

Thereby, in default of a contract, it became his property, as the authors found when they brought up the question of profits after 'Salmagundi' had proved to be a little gold mine. 'All they ever received from him was a hundred dollars apiece, although at the time the original copyright expired in 1822, Paulding conjectures that he had made ten or perhaps fifteen thousand dollars out of it, probably an extravagant estimate.'* Whatever the rights of it may have been, Davie's duskiness cost him the life of the goose that was laying the golden eggs. After twenty numbers, the concoctors of 'Salmagundi' decided that they had done enough for his pocket, and the performance ended as abruptly as it had begun. Some ten years later Longworth is known to have been active in the publishing of plays, but his name will go down with 'Salmagundi.'

Irving learned something from the connection. When two years later he had dashed off his burlesque 'History of New York,' he took out his own copyright, put the book through the press in Philadelphia, and virtually acted as his own publisher. Though the work was advertised on December 6th, 1809, as 'this day published by Inskeep and Bradford, No. 128 Broadway,' a letter from Irving to Brevoort in relation to the forthcoming publication of the 'Sketch Book' says: 'When I published the first edition of "Knickerbocker" I only allowed Bradford and Inskeep 20 pr.ct. and they take all the risk of the work's not selling.' The method of paying a royalty to the

* Pierre Irving, 'Life of Irving.'

author was still far off. Irving, like Cooper, during most of his life kept many of the functions of bookmaking in his own hands. In England he sold the copyrights for what he could get—only priority of publication gave them value. At home he sold editions of so many copies, or the rights for a certain number of years. The professional publisher (let me repeat) hardly emerged as a separate entity in the book trade till the second quarter of the century. The Harpers were primarily printers. The Wileys, Putnams, and Appletons were booksellers.

Wood and Wiley are among the earliest New York names that survive in the publishing business to-day. Samuel Wood was a country schoolmaster till past forty, when he decided there was not a decent living for his family in teaching, and came to New York. He set up a little second-hand bookshop on Pearl Street, where the city book trade centred, and sold books and stationery and for awhile drygoods. But this could not satisfy the ex-pedagogue. He had theories about a field for better books for children, and decided to make his own. So he set up a small press and proceeded to turn out a long list of primers and little books, many of them written, as well as printed, published, and sold, by himself. And according to tradition he was in the habit of carrying them in his pockets and giving them away as tidbits to children. They were tiny affairs. Wood prospered, the business grew. He presently took two sons into the firm, published a Quaker magazine, 'The Friend of Peace,' and opened a branch in Baltimore. For half a century after its founding the house of Wood continued to sell books as well as to publish textbooks and medical works. In the 1860's these miscellaneous activities were abandoned for the special business of handling medical and scientific publications. The Woods sponsored and published the 'Medical Record' and other journals and have ever since been prominent in the publication of medical books and periodicals, the firm name surviving as "William Wood and Company." Much the same thing happened to the house of Wiley, which eventually abandoned the publication of books of 'pure literature' in order to specialize in scientific and technical books. But the original Wiley—or rather the first two Wileys, Charles and John—are intimately concerned with the story of American belles-lettres during the first half of the nineteenth century.

The house of Wiley, like the house of Wood, has done business under the same name for more than a century. It was founded in 1807, and therefore celebrates this year its 125th anniversary. Irving's 'Salmagundi' appeared in that year, and no doubt was on sale at Charles Wiley's bookshop in Reade Street. That was 'way down town, but so was all of the New York that mattered, in those days. Charles Wiley had been born and brought up in the neighborhood. His father John Wiley was a New Yorker of note. He lived on a large plot of land leased from old Trinity, lying between the church and the river. His house was just behind the rear wall of the churchyard; his distillery was nearer the river. There he made a fortune in the approved pre-Revolutionary manner, owning a fleet of brigs and schooners which plied profitably in the rum-slaves-and-molasses trade that was also enriching Puritan New England. Early in the Revolution he equipped a company for active service, became its captain, and later a major actively serving in the Revolutionary army. He was a useful citizen and an ardent Whig, was of the party that tore down the statue of George III in the Bowling Green in 1781. He once bore a challenge to Alexander Hamilton from the Colonel Oswald who had fought with Matthew Carey. Major John Wiley was a bluff and crusted citizen of the old school, loved his quarrel and would have his way. On the authority of one of his descendants, 'his wife once refused to sign a deed which he wished to have executed, and he threatened to hold his finger in the flame of a lighted candle until she consented. He did so and for the rest of his life had a crooked finger; but my grandmother signed the deed. . . . He was well educated, vastly more patriotic than amiable, loved his friends devotedly, hated his enemies fervently, used a great deal of bad language and old Jamaica. He was an honest man, a brave soldier, a true patriot.'

Charles Wiley was twenty-five when he began as a bookseller. He seems to have been at school or at leisure during the age when most of his contemporaries in the book trade were serving as shop-boys or apprentices. Perhaps he went to Columbia; certainly his clients recognized him as a man of education and

New York Arrives 157

taste. No doubt his father the Major started him in business when he was ready for it. He was primarily a bookseller, though he owned a printing press at some time during the early years; and would later become publisher of some of the earliest American books of high literary quality.

Up to 1815 or even later American imprints are confusing. 'Published by' seems to have been used casually as an equivalent of 'printed for.' Often (as in eighteenth century England) a book was issued as 'printed for' a number of booksellers, who presumably shared the risks of publication. Till about 1830 most of the Harper books bore on the title-page merely 'printed by J. & J. Harper'; soon after, without apparent consciousness of radical change, the Harper imprints read 'published by' or 'printed and published by.' The Harpers were primarily printers. A bookseller sponsoring a new publication was naturally more likely to call himself publisher on the imprint. But the general usage was haphazard. One of the earliest books to bear the Wiley name was a 'Life of Wellington' issued in 1814 with the imprint: 'Printed and Published by Van Winkle and Wiley, Wall and New Streets, New York.' But 'Travels in Egypt,' a year later, was 'Published by Jacob Gillet, Van Winkle and Wiley, Printers.' Van Winkle was a printer by trade, Wiley a bookseller. These two had some sort of partnership for a few years. But in 1819, when Fitz-Greene Halleck's 'Fanny' was 'published by C. Wiley and Co.,' Van Winkle can hardly have been the 'Co.'; for that year Irving's 'Sketch Book' was 'printed by C. S. Van Winkle' alone. Wiley probably gave the work to Van Winkle and was its unnamed publisher: a letter of Halleck's supplies the evidence. Halleck was one of the reading and writing men (*literati* was the word) who already found a pleasant gathering-place at Wiley's bookshop. Charles Wiley was the sort of bookseller that makes his clients feel at home and shares their interest in bookish matters. Halleck was among the New Yorkers exiled by the yellow fever epidemic of 1819, and whiled away his days in the country by writing a string of satirical verses called 'Fanny.' He would naturally have mentioned them to his friend Wiley, on his return to the city; and at the end of the year wrote to his sister: 'I have spun out the poem which I repeated to you last summer into a book of fifty pages. . . . I had no intention of publishing it, but the bookseller who brought out Irving's "Sketch Book" offering to publish "Fanny" in a style similar to that work, I consented to his doing so. . . . The bookseller stated to me that I was the only writer in America, Irving excepted, whose work he would risk publishing.' The opinion was founded partly on his judgment of 'Fanny' and partly on the popularity of the 'Croaker Papers,' which, acknowledged by Drake and Halleck, had just been issued in an unauthorized edition, and were as popular as Irving's 'Salmagundi' had been a dozen years before.

Charles Wiley presently published 'Fanny,' and

was clearly the bookseller mentioned as having 'brought out' the 'Sketch Book.' There is a clue to his connection with it in Pierre Irving's 'Life'; though the biographer does not see the meaning of his own evidence. Here and elsewhere (like Lounsbury and others) he confounds Charles Wiley and his son John. The numbers of the 'Sketch Book,' of course, were written in England. From London, Irving wrote to his friend Brevoort asking him to arrange for the publication of the sketches here. Irving had been acting as a sort of agent in London for Moses Thomas the Philadelphia bookseller. Thomas seems to have been unable to meet certain obligations incurred for him, and Irving did not now feel like turning the 'Sketch Book' over to him as publisher, though he wished him to have preference as a bookseller. 'I wish,' he wrote Brevoort, 'the copyright secured for me, and the work printed and then sold to one or more booksellers, who will take the whole impression at a fair discount, and give cash or good notes for it. This makes short work of it, and is more profitable to the author than selling the copyright.' Brevoort apparently turned the matter over to Wiley, and Wiley placed the book with his friend Van Winkle. Irving was much pleased with Van Winkle's work, and 'Bracebridge Hall' went to him also, though Irving again had thoughts of Moses Thomas as publisher. Whatever his temporary delinquency may have been, Thomas was a respectable and successful man, and Irving and he were life-long friends.

If chance failed to set Charles Wiley's name on the title-page of the 'Sketch Book,' chance or merit very soon associated him with an equally famous author and work. Traveling on his ordinary business through western New York in 1820, Wiley made an agreeable acquaintance, a country gentleman named Cooper whose family hailed from up-state, though he was then living at Mamaroneck. Cooper had already published a book, his early stunt-novel 'Precaution.' But it had been issued anonymously, and Wiley knew nothing of its authorship. When Cooper presently wrote 'The Spy,' he naturally offered it to the New York bookseller with whom he had passed some pleasant hours on the road, and whose shop he had very likely visited after their meeting. Wiley was receptive, he would print the book and put his name to it; but he would not pay cash for the copyright. It was the only time any publisher ever got the chance to buy a Fenimore Cooper novel. For 'The Spy' succeeded beyond hope, and Cooper thereafter, like Irving, chose to keep his copyrights in his own hands. Cooper indeed had the habit of attending to the actual manufacture of his books. He bought the paper, hired the printer, saw his book through the press, and showed a general distrust of professional publishers. As against selling outright, or accepting a percentage of the profits, he preferred taking the whole risk of profit and loss. Copyright for 'The Spy' and its successors was recorded in Wiley's name, but this simply to preserve the anonymity of 'the author of "Precaution."' The imprint of 'The Spy' reads: 'New York: Wiley and Halsted, 3 Wall-Street. William Grattan, Printer.' This Halsted was probably the 'Co.' of the 'Fanny' imprint. Charles Wiley's mother was a Halsted, and the several Halsteds associated with the Wiley firm at intervals for many years were cousins or connections. The second and enlarged edition of Halleck's 'Fanny' had the Wiley and Halsted imprint. Cooper's 'Pioneers,' 'Pilot,' and 'Lionel Lincoln' bore the name of Charles Wiley alone, with various printers.

'The Spy' was an experiment; no wonder Charles Wiley failed to jump at it. The 'Waverley Novels' were just then at the top of their popularity. What chance did American materials offer an American romancer? Cooper himself had little faith in the book, and left the first volume lying about for some time before he began the second. Its printing began before the end was in sight, and Charles Wiley, as the copy rolled in, was troubled lest the book run altogether beyond reasonable limits; whereupon Cooper supplied a closing chapter which was at once printed and paged, leaving the romancer to fit his tale into the intervening space as best he might. Cooper, living in the country, had no chance to read the proofs. Even an author who camped next door to his printer must correct his proofs piecemeal, without chance of revision, since the chapters were printed and the type broken up as the book went on. His only recourse from gross errors was the list of errata—a clumsy afterthought.

A letter to Cooper from Charles Wiley, when

'The Spy' came out, throws light on their friendly relations, as well as on the small scale by which success was measured at that time. ' "The Spy" has succeeded over and beyond my expectations, and they were not easily to be exceeded. We have sold 100 to M. Carey & Lea, 100 to Lockwood, each at six months, 50 to Gilley at three months, besides 24 copies to several others. We have also retailed a very considerable number ourselves. A number of copies have been sold or sent on commission to the principal towns in different States. We have sold and sent off on commission about 600 copies, and think it probable the whole edition will be sold in three months.' Wiley goes on to give some of the opinions he has had of 'The Spy,' mainly approving: Halleck was especially delighted with it. And a postscript indicates that Charles Wiley's father the Major was still very much alive: 'I forgot to mention that my father read "The Spy," and is so delighted that he proposes, on your arrival in "The Mamaroneck" [the stagecoach of that name] to take off the horses and with assistance of others to drag you throughout the city.'

Wiley's guess fell short. The first small edition was followed within four months by two others of three and five thousand copies. The American novel was on its way. England could not long delay recognition though the great John Murray refused 'The Spy,' as he had refused the 'Sketch Book,' till others had taken the risk of their first publication in England. Later on, England was disposed to claim that Cooper had been first encouraged there: which

THE SPY;

A TALE OF

THE NEUTRAL GROUND.

—◆—

"Breathes there a man with soul so dead,
Who never to himself hath said,
This is my own, my native land..."

—◆—

BY

THE AUTHOR OF "PRECAUTION."

———

IN TWO VOLUMES.

VOL. I.

———

NEW-YORK:

WILEY & HALSTED, 3, WALL-STREET.

Wm. Grattan, Printer.

1821.

THE FIRST GREAT AMERICAN NOVEL

New York Arrives 163

Cooper himself stoutly denied. American rights in England, at that time, had to be guarded by the same uncertain methods used for English books in America. Early sheets, simultaneous publication, 'author's editions,' strove for the crumbs that fell from the table. England, to be sure, was ready for a square deal some half-century before America would meet her with the necessary legislation.

During the early 1820's Wiley's bookshop became a rendezvous for bookish people, the Mermaid Tavern or the Old Corner of its place and time. There was a back room known as the Den, where the writing gentry of the city forgathered. Charles Wiley was host; Fenimore Cooper, now living in town, was the nerve-centre of the group. In the Den the 'Bread and Cheese Club,' or 'Cooper's,' came into being. Wiley habitués, with Wiley himself, were its charter members. To it belonged sooner or later Fitz-Greene Halleck and J. K. Paulding and Verplanck and Percival and later the Yankees S. F. B. Morse the painter and Bryant the poet and a young lawyer named Dana. It was a literary-convivial club noted for its dinners and its rational jollity, if there is such a thing. It met on stated evenings. By day Wiley's shop was still the gathering-place. One summer Cooper sailed almost daily from Hallett's Cove to the city, in his sloop *Van Tromp*, and often took his daughter Susan with him, 'resting until the turn of the tide at Mr. Wiley's bookstore.'*

* Cooper, 'Pages and Pictures.'

Working as apprentice or clerk in Charles Wiley's bookshop at that time was his oldest son John. Born in 1808, the boy had been well schooled up to the college age, and had then gone into his father's business. He grew up in the atmosphere of the Den, and never forgot the remarkable group that frequented it. He never forgot, it may be, that some of these genial gentlemen with their scribbling had cost his father a pretty penny. Charles Wiley seems to have been more successful as a host than as a man of business. His publishing, certainly, brought him no fortune. Though 'The Spy,' 'The Pioneers,' and 'The Pilot' were famous successes, there was no vast profit in them and the author was astute enough to bag most of what there was. Cooper's fourth novel, 'Lionel Lincoln,' was a failure. About then Charles Wiley's health was failing too, and by 1825 Cooper had to look elsewhere for a publisher. For Wiley's sake as well as his own, Cooper arranged with the Philadelphia Careys to take over his forthcoming book, 'The Last of the Mohicans.' Charles Wiley died, we know, in 1826, just as the 'Mohicans' was being issued under the imprint of H. C. Carey & I. Lea.

Soon after Wiley's death we find his son John, then just a man by law, fairly launched as a bookseller under his own name. By 1828 he had made an excellent connection as agent for Carey & Lea, who thus far held their advantage as general publishers over the oncoming Harpers of New York. John Wiley was New York agent also for Thomas Wardle of Philadelphia, by all odds the leading importer of English and foreign books for the American market. In 1832 John Wiley formed a partnership with George Long (another bookseller's son), and Wiley and Long did business together for a few years. In 1834 Fenimore Cooper's provocative 'Letter to His Countrymen' appeared under the imprint of John Wiley alone. According to the preliminary 'advertisement' the author has 'presented it to the son of his old and much esteemed publisher, Charles Wiley, who has given it its present form for purposes connected with his own convenience.' Osborn and Buckingham were the printers: John Wiley (unlike Charles) does not seem to have been a printer at any time. The 'Letter' cannot have been a valuable gift in a money way; it is of interest as the first book that bore Fenimore Cooper's name on the title-page. John Wiley's was there with it.

XII

WILEYS AND PUTNAMS

WILEY AND LONG were associated for some years as booksellers, publishers, and distributors for the Philadelphia firms of Carey, Lea & Blanchard and Carey & Hart. With them, by 1838, was a young man of a name fated to become mighty in the publishing field. In 1840 Long withdrew and a new firm came into being, Wiley and Putnam. For a decade the records of the Wileys and Putnams are inextricable.

John Wiley the senior member of the firm was a man of good sense, conservative by nature and inclined to play safe in a business that had proved treacherous for his father's sanguine temper. Young George Palmer Putnam, with no such background of experience, was full of ideas and ambitions. Born at Brunswick, Maine, in 1814, at eleven he was living prentice-fashion in the house of a Boston uncle who had a carpet-store. Detesting carpets and the rigor of a Puritan household, he headed for New York at fifteen and found a job in a little bookshop on Broadway near Maiden Lane, at $25.00 a year and board. The master of the shop, G. W. Bleecker, published one of the flimsy, pretentious periodicals of the time, 'The Euterpiad, an Album of Music, Poetry and

Prose.' 'An apprenticeship of a year or two,' says Putnam in an autobiographical fragment, 'in this little mart of school-books, Andover theology, albums, stationery, and cheap pictures, was not a severe ordeal.' He read the best stuff he could get hold of. After his year or two with Bleecker he made a better connection as general clerk for Jonathan Leavitt. Theological and religious books were still a leading branch of the book trade, and Leavitt specialized in them. He was a Yankee bookbinder who had come to New York to look out for the book department of Mr. Daniel Appleton, a dry-goods merchant. They were brothers-in-law. The book department flourished, but for some reason Leavitt chose, after a year or so, to set up for himself.

We have a sweeping view of the American book trade in the 1830's in the fragment of autobiography left by the original Putnam:

'At this time (1832-1833) the chief publishers of the land were these: In Boston, Lincoln and Edmunds (succeeded by Gould and Lincoln), devoted especially to the views of the Baptists; Crocker and Brewster, the leading orthodox Congregationalist publishers; Cummings and Hilliard, afterwards Hilliard, Gray and Co., chiefly engaged in schoolbooks; Lilly, Wait and Co., reprinters of foreign reviews, etc.; R. P. and C. Williams, respectably rusty in the general trade; Allen and Ticknor, predecessors of the present firm of Ticknor and Fields; Little, Brown . . .

'In New York T. and J. Swords, the ancient Episcopal booksellers in Broadway, whose imprint may be found dated as early as 1792; Evert Duyckinck, an estimable man, father of the well-known authors E. A. and G. L. Duyckinck; S. Wood and Sons (the sons worthily continuing) and J. B. Collins in the school-book and jobbing trade; Elam Bliss, the gentlemanly and popular caterer on Broadway, whose elegant little "Talisman," edited by Bryant, Verplanck, and Robert C. Sands, was the father of American "annuals," and a good deal better than some of the children; G. and C. Carvill, the English successors of the still more famous Eastburn, on the corner of Wall Street and Broadway, the most exclusive dealers in general literature and, like Bliss's opposite, the lounging place of the *literati*; George Dearborn, then a new star, issuing double column Byrons, Johnsons, Burkes, besides "The American Monthly," "The Republic of Letters," and "The New York Review," Jonathan Leavitt taking charge especially of the department of theology; and the brothers Harper were holding up their gigantic business of producing general literature, then consisting chiefly of reprints of English authors.

'In Philadelphia this main branch of the trade was then largely in control of Carey and Lea, successors of the famous Matthew Carey, in the premises still occupied by Blanchard and Lea, the leading medical publishers. Carey and Hart, in the same "corner of Fourth and Chesnut," rivaled the Harpers in their dispensation of new novels, and also in more solid literature. . . .

'In Andover, Mass., Mr. Flagg printed the learned works of Moses Stuart and Leonard Woods. In Hartford "Uncle Silas" Andrus would grind out cords of Shakespeares, Byrons, Bunyans, and "Alonzo and Melissas," suited for the country trade. In Springfield the Merriams printed Chitty's law books and others, but had not yet begun to work the golden mine of Webster's "Unabridged." Here and there a book would come along with the imprint of Hyde of Portland, Kay of Pittsburg, Howe of New Haven, Metcalf of Cambridge, Gould of Albany, Armstrong of Baltimore; but the three great cities first named, then as now, monopolized the bulk of the bookmaking—Boston rather leading the van.'

So it was that the elderly George Palmer Putnam recalled the personnel of the book trade when he was a very young trader. His memories are not altogether accurate, but his general picture is vivid. Conditions were not wholly satisfactory in the publishing trade: they never have been and never will be. In 1932 we have seen much agitation and heart-searching among members of the craft; and some remarkably gloomy views have been expressed. In 1832 a book was published in London the title-page of which read: 'Bibliophobia: Remarks on the Present Languid and Depressed State of Literature and the Book-trade. In a Letter Addressed to the Author of "Bibliomania." By Mercurius Rusticus. With Notes by Cato Parvus.'

No doubt in 2032 . . .

The young G. P. Putnam who became John Wiley's partner in 1838 had strong convictions and plenty of energy. A year earlier, while he was still a clerk with Wiley and Long, he was chosen secretary of a new society for the establishment of an international copyright law. It was the beginning of a campaign so long that he did not live to see it through. John Wiley also was among the first and most persistent advocates of a copyright law. Putnam no sooner became Wiley's partner than he began to push for expansion. He believed a branch business in England would be a good thing for American books over there as well as for English books in America. In London, too, he would be able to work in the interests of a copyright law. It was agreed that he should take charge of a bookshop there and try the theory out. He found a place in the classic street for bookshops, Paternoster Row. According to a description by James Brown of Little & Brown, it was not an impressive centre at that time: 'Paternoster Row I was greatly disappointed in. Instead of a street full of splendid booksellers' shops, it is a narrow lane barely admitting a carriage: dirty, dark, gloomy and disgusting. It is for the most part filled with booksellers; but what gives character to the whole lane is a large tallow-chandler's establishment, and the beef market. In this mean street, however, are sold more fine books than in any other in the world. Here, too, booksellers with their families live and here as elsewhere in London you meet the bookseller's wife assisting in the labors of the shop and busy with the pen, or assorting parcels for distant customers, and in discussing the comparative value of the different editions of Boyle and Dumas.' Perhaps Putnam the American found the street too stuffy: he moved presently to Waterloo Place. His business was mainly exporting English books and periodicals. He tried to sell American books to English readers, but his imported editions had to compete with English reprints. Like Fenimore Cooper and others before and after him, he was continually irritated by the general British ignorance and misunderstanding of American conditions and affairs. In 1845, when he had been in London several years, he published a book of 300 pages called: 'American Facts: Notes and Statistics Relating to the Government, Resources, Engagements, Manufactures, Commerce, Religion, Education, Literature, Fine Arts, Manners and Customs of the United States of America.'

Sweeping enough! The young bookseller was popular in London and had made many English friends; but their condescension to things American was more than he could easily endure. They professed contempt for American books—and stole them freely. 'American Facts' gives a list of 382 American books printed in England from 1841 to 1846, ranging all the way from theology to juveniles. There are sixty-odd books of fiction in the lot, and a dozen books of poetry. 'These lists,' says Putnam quietly, 'might have been used as a convenient answer to the query quoted from Sydney Smith: "Who reads an American book?"' Putnam's book got more of a hearing than Cooper's 'Notions of the Americans' had twenty years earlier, for it ran into several editions, or printings.*

During his seven years in London, Putnam had the entrée to the best literary society. He hobnobbed with Sergeant Talfourd and Thomas Campbell and Tom Moore. Washington Irving was a guest at his 'Knickerbocker Cottage.' The plan of a collected edition of Irving, to be issued by Wiley and Putnam, was broached then, though it would not be undertaken for some years. Putnam sent home frequent letters to the New York journals about English people and affairs. He was full of interest in British politics, the corn laws, the tariff, Ireland. He was much concerned about Pennsylvania's repudiation of her bonds, as well as about the raising of the Union Jack in the Sandwich Islands. Meanwhile he gave proof of his honest desire to see fair play in the matter of authors' rights on both sides of the Atlantic. If not its originator (and the point is obscure) he was among the first to recommend and to practice a method of royalty payment. In 1844 he proposed to Elizabeth Barrett to issue her poems in New York 'at his own risk and give her ten per cent on the profit.'

* The casual use of the word 'editions' was challenged by Jared Sparks at just that time (1843) in a private letter: 'Prescott and Bancroft publish what are called "editions," 500 each. They think there is some advantage in it, though where there are stereotype plates one can hardly see the propriety of calling each impression a new edition. . . . I have never adopted this mode.' Nearly a century later this confusion still exists. Even rare book dealers and collectors fail to distinguish clearly between editions, issues, and printings or impressions.

This was not the same thing as the true royalty payment of a percentage on the retail price. But it was a proposal almost incredible to Miss Barrett. 'Not that I ever asked for such a thing,' she said, reporting the strange affair to Robert Browning: 'They were the terms offered. And I always considered the "percentage" as quite visionary—put in for the sake of effect, to make the agreement look better. But no— you see! One's poetry has a real "commercial value" if you do but take it far enough away from the civilization of Europe.' She had just 'miraculously received' a remittance from Wiley & Putnam in New York. Browning was impressed, and praised the American publishers as 'fine fellows, who do a really straightforward un-American thing.' He saw indeed some glimmerings on the horizon of these benighted States: 'I like the progress of these Americans in taste, their amazing leaps like grasshoppers up to the sun—from—what is the from? what depth, do you remember, say ten or twelve years back—to Carlyle, and Tennyson, and—you! So, children, leave off Jack of Cornwall, and go on just to Homer!' Some of the leaping belonged to the poet's fancy rather than to American taste, for the 1830's, at least, had shown a remarkable demand here for the best English books, if the importations and piracies advertised in publishers' lists of the time are evidence.

Putnam must have had a way with him, for even Carlyle the crabbed took to him: 'a very intelligent, modest, and reputable-looking fellow.' Putnam offered him a true royalty arrangement, one of the first on record—ten per cent 'on the selling price of all the copies of "Cromwell" sent into the market by them'—and also on reprinted editions of his former works, or some of them. Such an offer was a marvel to the sage of Chelsea as well as to the poetess of Wimpole Street. He wellnigh chirps over it in a letter giving his friend Emerson the surprising news. The Boston firm of Little & Brown, with whom Emerson had placed a number of Carlyle's books, had been unable to make a profit out of them in competition with unauthorized editions from Philadelphia and New York. Meanwhile the stay-at-home partner John Wiley was doing an active business in New York. George Haven Putnam says that he was mainly a bookseller; but during those years of George Palmer Putnam's absence, Wiley published much of the best American literary work of the period. The Wiley and Putnam 'Library of American Books,' unlike most assemblies of the kind, contained original material of high importance, Poe's 'Tales' and 'The Raven,' Hawthorne's 'Mosses from an Old Manse,' Melville's 'Typee.'

The London branch of Wiley & Putnam was given up in 1847, and soon afterward the firm was dissolved. There was disparity of temperament between the partners, and there must have been frequent differences of opinion. Putnam's London experiment had not been highly profitable, and perhaps the conservative Wiley preferred freedom to play safe. George Haven Putnam thought it a pity his father and John Wiley had not stayed together, as each was in some fashion the complement of the other. They parted amicably enough, and the property was divided. Putnam kept most of the purely literary material except Ruskin, whom Wiley continued to publish for many years. Ruskin was among the famous writers (a notable instance to-day is Upton Sinclair) who have refused to make use of the offices of a professional publisher. Ruskin employed an agent to look out for details, but got out his own editions, and booksellers had to buy of him direct, at a very small discount from the retail price. Moreover Ruskin was a frank hater of America and her ways. Wiley had a very short reply from him to a letter proposing the issuance here of an authorized edition, on terms such as Carlyle had readily accepted. Ruskin seems to have simply washed his hands of the plan. Under the conditions Wiley felt justified in going ahead, and his reprints of Ruskin were excellent specimens of the bookmaking of that period. But after his separation from Putnam, Wiley undertook little new publication in the field of belles-lettres. Soon he was concentrating upon the scientific and technical works which ever since have been the specialty of the house. In 1875 the firm became John Wiley & Sons and under that style has built up the great business it is known for to-day.

Men of letters have always a tendency to overstress the importance of 'pure literature' in relation to the total mass of books written and published. In fact the existence or non-existence of creative or imaginative writing does not affect the production or value of scientific and technical writing. If the one deeply influences the moral and spiritual conduct of the world, the other equally influences its intellectual and material progress. Even the early colonial booksellers made as much as they could of the practical and scientific output of their time, a steadily growing store of fact and technology. During the years, a century ago, when we were developing a literature of our own, our lack of copyright laws made the publishing of such material increasingly precarious. A president of The Macmillan Co. remarked that 'the most inclusive new feature of the century seems to be the tendency of our larger publishers to widen the class of their publications so as to include school, technical and medical books. For in such books rather than in miscellaneous publications seem to lie at present the surest financial rewards of the publisher.' Since that was said, the rapid increase in scientific knowledge and technical invention has doubled and redoubled the output of technical books till they have reached a scale of which the purely literary writer and reader have no conception. The book review departments of the magazines and the newspapers deal almost entirely with the 'miscellaneous publications,' the books of fiction, poetry, biography, in which the gamble of publishing lies. Meanwhile a great and successful book industry goes on, untouched by these organs of criticism and opinion, untroubled by the problems of the publisher of belles-lettres, or the speculator in 'best-sellers.'

The 'Library of American Books' was rather too choice for its public. Its editor, Evert A. Duyckinck, was a stickler for quality and did not care about the little matter of marketability which publishers, willy-nilly, have to bear in mind. The 'Library' was not a popular success; but Putnam took it over and kept it going for awhile after separating from Wiley. In 1848 he published separately a book of verse that won a remarkable hearing and is not yet forgotten, Lowell's 'Fable for Critics.' As an anonymous skit Lowell thought well to turn it over to his friend Charles F. Briggs for publication in New York, rather than to have it issued in Boston. The jingle, full of lively hits at the expense of Lowell's fellow-authors, made an unexpected sensation, and ran to several editions in a short time. Some odd things happened to the title-page. Like the preface, it was written in the metre of the main poem. The earliest issue omitted a line and so spoiled sound and sense. The fourth issue of the second edition was marked by a still worse 'boner' on the publisher's part. Since the book came out Putnam had moved, and the title substituted '10 Park Place' for 'Broadway,' in the closing lines:

SET FORTH IN
October, the 21st day, in the year '48:
G. P. PUTNAM, BROADWAY

Lowell made amusing comment on this, many years later: 'Mr. Putnam, I believe, never discovered that the title-page was in metre, nor that it was in rhyme either. Mr. Norton told me the other day that he had a copy of some later edition in which the imprint was: "G. P. Putnam, Astor [or Something] Place." I don't remember whether I knew of it at the time, but had I known, I should have let it pass as adding to the humor of the book.' This is all very well, but where was C. F. Briggs, to whom Lowell had made a free gift of the book; an experienced editor who must have in some fashion seen the book through the press? G. P. Putnam was not often caught napping. Many of his ambitious schemes prospered. He dared to take over Irving's complete works and made a good deal of money for himself and the author, after the Careys had pronounced those works dead. He vanishes here from the limited stage of this book: the further story of G. P. Putnam's Sons being a story of steady growth in the field of general publishing, down to our time. The house of Putnam, moreover, has never ceased to function as bookseller.

Apart from his reputation as a publisher and bookseller, G. P. Putnam must in the end be remembered for his services to the cause of international copyright. He began to fight for it as a very young man, and he kept on fighting for it till his death. The battle was not won for nearly twenty years after he fell, and up to the last moment before the enactment of a proper (if not perfect) copyright law in 1891, the same basic conditions obtained that had so severely handicapped American publishing in the 1830's. In 1886 Dana Estes of Boston testified that it was useless to think of publishing the new work of an American author with any expectation of profit: he had given it up. And in 1891, just before the passage of the law, Brander Matthews wrote: 'Under the present "cut-throat" competition, the publishers of the works of such authors as Howells, James, Aldrich, Bret Harte and other leading American writers, have practically given up the attempt to compete with the unpaid-for reprints of foreign writers.'

The length of the struggle was due to the strong opposition not only of dull politicians, and of the papermakers headed by Cyrus Field of Atlantic Cable memory, but of some of the most prominent publishers, including Henry Carey Baird and the Harpers. With Baird it was a matter of honest if fallacious theory. With the rest it was a plain matter of 'business is business.'

XIII

APPLETONS AND HARPERS

DANIEL APPLETON, founder of one of the great New York publishing houses that have survived, was, like G. P. Putnam, an ambitious Yankee who saw his opportunity in the rapidly growing city beyond the New England border. He had been a dry-goods merchant in Haverhill as early as 1813, had moved to Boston in 1817, and eight years later transferred his business to New York. The year 1825 was a bad year there. The city had grown too fast, times were hard and jobs few. But the numbers were there, and a potential market larger than Boston or Philadelphia offered. D. Appleton opened a shop in Exchange Place, a good part of the town. His customers were among the best people of the city. He carried a few books, and found a demand for them; so he induced his brother-in-law Jonathan Leavitt, a bookbinder of Andover in Massachusetts, to take charge of a real book department. A year or two later Leavitt set up a book business of his own, and it was not long before Appleton dropped his dry-goods and became exclusively a bookseller and publisher. There seems to have been no quarrel between the two, for Appleton's son William served Leavitt as a clerk (with G. P. Putnam) before being taken into his father's business as a partner. After a few years' experience as a bookseller at wholesale and retail, Appleton made a tentative first step as publisher by issuing one or two little books of devotion, bits taken from the Bible, which found some sale. Then in 1832 the cholera came to New York; and Appleton turned it to profit by publishing 'A Refuge in Time of Plague and Pestilence,' another book of pious extracts whose title carried it through several editions. From that time on, the list of Appleton publications grew steadily in numbers and range, though little attempt was made to compete with the Careys and Harpers in the field of pure literature. The son William H. Appleton went several times to England to arrange for American editions of popular English gift-books and religious books. Another agent, blind Edward L. Youmans, went abroad repeatedly for Appleton as literary adviser, and bagged for the house the works of the great new scientific writers, Darwin, Spencer, Huxley, and Tyndall, as well as their contemporaries in Europe.

Appleton later built up a great business in subscription books and 'table books,' like Bryant's 'Picturesque America'—there was a vast market for that kind of publication in our America of the black-walnut period. In 1848 D. Appleton retired in favor of his four sons, especially directing that the firm name of D. Appleton & Co. should never be changed. It was after the elder Appleton left the firm that the great bulk of the house's business led to the establishment of a large printing plant in Brooklyn; so that the process by which the Harpers advanced from printers to publishers and booksellers was exactly reversed in the case of the Appletons. Later the Appleton printing plant was given up, when modern methods of specialization led to a general separation of the business of printing from the business of publishing.

Harper is another name that has kept its place in the annals of American bookmaking for more than a century. Beginning as printers, after the older colonial tradition, the Harpers became booksellers and publishers by a natural process of development and expansion. They continued to do job printing for many years after they had begun to issue books under their own name. The four brothers were sons of a Long Island carpenter, farmer, and shop-keeper. James, the eldest (born in 1795), had no intention of being a rural jack-at-all-trades. At sixteen he was a printer's apprentice in New York, and his brother John soon followed him there. They were virtuous apprentices of the copybook order. They ardently practiced the industry and thrift laid down by Poor Richard and the other eighteenth century moralists. A fellow-apprentice, Thurlow Weed, long afterward paid tribute to young James Harper's well-nigh inhuman zeal for work: 'It was the rule of his life to study not how little he could work, but how much. Often, after a good day's work, he would say to me, "Thurlow, let's break the back of another token [250 impressions]—just break its back." I would generally consent reluctantly "just to break the back" of the token; but James would beguile me, or laugh at my complaints, and never let me off till the token was completed, fair and square. It was a custom with us in summer to do a fair half-day's work before the other boys and men got their breakfast. James and I would meet by appointment in the gray of the morning and go down to the printing-room. . . .' Bear for work though he was (and stickler for piety—none of the Harpers ever did a stroke of work on Sunday), James Harper is reputed to have been a cheerful soul, fond of telling stories, and equipped with a dry humor of the Lincolnian strain. Physically he was tall and strong, temperamentally a 'born mixer,' attending off-hand to what would now be called the industrial relations of the Harper concern.

J. & J. Harper set up business as printers in 1817, with two younger brothers as compositors. Their first book was an edition of Seneca's 'Morals.' It was 'Published by Evert Duyckinck, J. & J. Harper (printers).' J. & J. Harper was the common style of the firm in the 1820's, and 'Printed by J. & J. Harper' still stood on their title-pages after they had begun to be publishers on a considerable scale. The title of their edition of Bulwer's 'Devereux' (1829) reads 'Printed by J. & J. Harper, 82 Cliff Street'; and this heads the list of advertisements preceding the text, 'Popular Works, Recently Printed by'—etc. But the page heading of the list has 'Works Recently Published,' and a year or so later 'Published by' begins to appear regularly on Harper imprints. The 'Devereux' list is interesting. Its fifty items are mainly reprints of English work, Scott, Gibbon, Robertson, the Misses Porter, and many lighter books now long forgotten. There are only two or three of even probable American source. Bear in mind that before 1830 there was little American literary material worth printing except Irving and Cooper, Halleck's 'Fanny,' and one little book of poems by Bryant. But much of the English stuff Harper was reprinting was negligible from the modern point of view.

The firm name became Harper & Brothers in 1833, and has stood unchanged for a century. By then they had built up a large business without much traffic with authors. They were the first publishers to adopt stereotyping as a regular practice. They began in the 1830's the first of a long series of omnibus reprints—forerunners, in cheap form, of our 'Everyman' and 'Modern' libraries. The four brothers were a marvelous team, working together from first to last in perfect harmony, and with a division of responsibilities that seems to have satisfied everybody. John Harper was the man of detail, looked out for finances and accounts, bought supplies, and oversaw the Harper typography. When the establishment was burned in 1853 (with most of Herman Melville's books and other stock of great value) it was John who took the lead in carrying on. The brothers had then plenty of money to retire on, and there were younger members of the family to take up the burden of a fresh start. But John Harper could not see himself and his brothers laid on the shelf. 'We must show them that we are not old fogies,' he said; and proceeded to design and build the new fireproof quarters of Harper & Brothers in Franklin Square. He was nicknamed 'the Colonel,' and was the sportsman of the family out of business hours, with a special fondness for fast horses.

The third brother, Joseph Wesley, was the literary man of the four, a man of wide reading and good taste. All manuscripts came to him, and he attended to personal dealings with authors. These last, as we have seen, were not matters of immense commercial importance to the Harpers. Their prosperity was largely founded on the lack of an international copyright law, and they (the original four) were from first to last opposed to the enactment of such a law. The list of 'Harper's Library of Select Novels,' cheap reprints in paper, in 1842 reached 615 volumes, all but about half a dozen being foreign books, largely contemporary. A generation later the 'Seaside Library' and the 'Franklin Square Library' were issuing at ten and twenty cents the best new work of English novelists. The family chronicler of the Harpers naturally does not stress this aspect of the Harper history. He says with complaisance that it was the custom to get advanced sheets for 'authorized editions' from the foreign publishers, 'and to pay for them, under the protection of trade courtesy. The system was but a makeshift, but it usually answered its purpose, and its principles were respected by all first-class publishing houses.'* The cynic might describe this usage as a sort of honor among thieves. Henry Holt found a more seemly formula for it as 'a brief realization of the ideals of philosophical anarchism—self-regulation without law.' J. Henry Harper stresses the payment to Dickens by the Harpers of £1,250 for 'Great Expectations,' to Thackeray of £400 for 'The Virginians,' and of respectable sums to Trollope and George Eliot and Wilkie Collins: 'These arrangements were satisfactory, with few exceptions, to English authors, and were usually sought by them.' Naturally—since it was a case of that or nothing.

That the 'gentlemen's agreement' did not always hold is suggested by the evidence of another family chronicler, George Haven Putnam: alas, his testimony is at the Harpers' expense. It seems that in 1851 the Swedish authoress Frederika Bremer came over here to lecture, and the Putnams thought it a good time to get out an American edition of her works. They arranged with her accordingly, and printed two volumes which had remarkable success here; whereupon some other publishers, including the Harpers, announced competing editions. Putnam remonstrated, and took Miss Bremer to see the Harpers, where she was welcomed with much courtesy. But when the interview was over, and Putnam appealed to her hosts for fair treatment, he was blandly informed that courtesy was courtesy and business was business. There was no ruthlessness of this kind to be charged

* Harper, 'House of Harper.'

against the later generations of Harpers: it was a survival of a ruder age.

The fourth brother among these old Trojans, Fletcher Harper, was a quiet gentleman of great administrative talent, a born manager and 'executive.' His hand kept control of the development and conduct of the great Harper 'plant,' in all matters of practical detail. He had the sharpness, the promptness, and the foresight of the big business man. He found his place in the establishment with the same ease and certainty that his older brothers had shown. The four worked together. When somebody once asked who was Harper and who the Brothers he was bidden to fill in any Christian name of the four as senior partner. By an odd chance, the last book published during the original partnership (broken only by death) was a new edition of Seneca's 'Morals'; the book to which J. & J. Harper had first put their names.

XIV

THE BOSTON RENAISSANCE

IN THE eighteenth century Boston had ceded its place as the chief centre of bookselling and publishing, first to Philadelphia and then to New York. In the nineteenth century it was to recover its position for awhile, thanks to a remarkable group of writers and a scarcely less remarkable group or series of publishers and booksellers. Little, Brown & Co. claim to be the oldest survivors among them, on the ground that they represent a continuous succession of booksellers who carried on the business founded by Ebenezer Battelle in 1784. But there were three changes of proprietorship before the end of the century, all under different names. Then for thirty years, from 1797 to 1827, the business belonged to W. P. and L. Blake, who did some publishing as well as sold books. In 1827 the business was bought by Hilliard, Gray & Co., the 'Co.' being Charles C. Little. Ten years later Little took over the concern in partnership with James Brown, who had been running the University Book Store at Cambridge. The firm name was Charles C. Little & Co., then Little & Brown, and finally (in 1847) Little, Brown & Co. For a long time the house specialized in law books. It published Jared Sparks's 'Life of Washington,' and

The Old Corner Book Store in Boston, About 1840.
From a Painting by M. Fuller

The Boston Renaissance 189

the works of Daniel Webster and Parkman. John Bartlett, a member of the firm, was the compiler of the standard 'Familiar Quotations.' Later the firm was successful in publishing many of the most popular American writers, and it has retained its faculty of picking winners to this day.

The 'Old Corner Book Store' is another Boston institution whose continuity is rather sentimental than exact. The building still stands, but the booksellers have deserted it, the last incumbents transferring the famous name, with a certain lack of humor, to a shop in the middle of a cross street. The 'Old Corner Book Store, Inc.' is some distance from the sign-beplastered building on the corner of Washington and School Streets—a landmark sadly defaced, but still extant, after being threatened with extinction for nearly a century. It was built in 1812, the year after the great fire destroyed most of the bookshops of Boston. Truth compels the admission that the patent-medicine signs now adorning it are not altogether out of place, since it was built by one Thomas Crease, an apothecary; and it was still an apothecary shop when, nearly a century later, Timothy Carter took it over and made a bookshop of it. It was even then under sentence of destruction: its success as a bookshop seems to have given it a new lease of life. The story of Carter and Hendee has been a good deal bungled by various chroniclers. A letter written by Timothy Carter clears up the facts. It was written in 1894 to Damrell and Upham, then occupants of the Old Corner. Carter was a very old man, with a long-standing grudge and an excellent memory. 'In 1828,' he says, 'I took a lease of the whole estate for a term of six years and six months, at $2,000 a year: it was then yielding but $1,400. They would make it no longer than six and a half years because rich owners had determined to rebuild it at the end of that time, before which some change was to take place, but George W. Brimmer, with whom I negotiated the lease, agreed verbally, but would not have it expressed in the lease, that if they did then rebuild they would allow me to take away whatever I had put upon the estate and if not would negotiate some extension of the lease.

'Under this arrangement, I proceeded to remodel the estate, fitting the front store for a first class bookstore, as it is now. The floor of the front store was then three or four steps above the sidewalk. I lowered the floor and rebuilt the walls of the first story of the corner building new all round, making a handsome and convenient bookstore, and in the then vacant yard of the estate on School Street I erected new brick buildings as they now stand. Also on the deep land in rear of new buildings I erected a large wooden building, in which I had seven machine printing presses, at first run by a span of Canadian horses, and afterwards by steam. Four of them were Treadwell's new invention, which were subsequently taken to Brattleboro and run by the Connecticut River.

'I spent about seven thousand dollars upon the estate, bringing it to a rental value of many thousand dollars instead of the $1,400 a year and before the expiration of the lease, George Brimmer having died abroad, the owners leased to other parties without my knowledge, so the owners have for seventy years enjoyed the benefit of my engineering and expenditures under a six and a half years' lease without ever speaking with me of it; but whether they ever knew of the verbal agreement of George W. Brimmer with me in relation to it I know not.

'I was top and bottom of the whole matter until wholly under way, when I sold one-third to a younger brother, not then of age, and one-third to C. J. Hendee, a clerk, and myself retired under the name of Co. Soon the wholesale business of the firm had so increased that the retail department was sold to Allen & Ticknor, to whom J. T. Fields came in as an apprentice and subsequently became partner with Ticknor's son, succeeded by Dutton & Co., A. Williams, Cupples & Upham, and then by your firm of Damrell & Upham. This, gentlemen, gives a general idea of the Old Corner Bookstore from the start.

'The second story of the new buildings erected by me on School Street were first occupied by S. G. Goodrich with his literary enterprises and assistants, and the third story by I. R. Butts, an accomplished printer, whose type office was connected with my press office.

'It was during my six and a half years' lease that the building became a point of literary attraction and convenience. It is a building of deep historical interest anyway, performing its use to mankind with no cessation from the days of Queen Anne; and I have a sense of pride in observing that my engineering and improvements under a six and a half years's lease was so judicious as to save the rich owners the necessity of building or of spending a dollar upon it for seventy years.'

Throughout all the period we are concerned with —that is, up to the middle of the nineteenth century—the Old Corner Book Store was at the centre of a colony of printers, bookbinders, and booksellers occupying School Street, Cornhill, and nearby Washington Street. Ticknor and Fields are the names that will always be identified with the Old Corner Book Store in its prime. William D. Ticknor was the son of a New Hampshire farmer. He came to Boston, very young, to enter the brokerage office of an uncle. But something drew him to the book trade, and in 1832, with a partner equally youthful, he took over the Old Corner premises and the retail business of Carter and Handee. After a year John Allen his partner withdrew, and the business ran on under Ticknor's name for a dozen years.

If the Old Corner had begun to be a literary rendezvous in Timothy Carter's time, its popularity grew fast during Ticknor's incumbency. He was warmly interested in imaginative writing, and now a group of authors were growing up to his hand. Holmes and Emerson, Lowell and Longfellow and Whittier, all came into his shop. He published some of their earlier books under his name alone. Among

The Boston Renaissance 193

his apprentices was another New Hampshire boy, James T. Fields, who lived for some time in the master's household, after the paternal custom that still held. He was a boy of great promise, and in 1845 Ticknor took him into the firm with another new member, John Reed. For a short time the house imprint became Ticknor, Reed & Fields. But Reed had brought nothing to the business but a little money, and soon withdrew. Ticknor and Fields, left to themselves, were a strong pair, and the story of their career as publishers of the best literature of their time is a part of our national history. But they were remarkable personalities, apart from their bookselling and publishing.

Ticknor was the solid man of the firm, a prominent citizen, director of this and treasurer of that. He had the courage of his convictions, too, in taking up new authors and new enterprises. Against Fields' judgment he bought the dying 'Atlantic Monthly,' and made a success of it. It was Ticknor, not Fields, for whom the shy, chill Hawthorne had one of his few warm attachments; though Fields had been the one to extract 'The Scarlet Letter' from that costive genius. Ticknor was the practical, stay-at-home member of the firm, while Fields did the traveling, coddled the authors, and was something of a man of letters in his own right. It was much the same situation as with Wiley & Putnam in New York, a little earlier. The later history of the Old Corner Book Store has been fully told. W. D. Ticknor died in 1864, his son succeeding him in the firm: a year later

Ticknor & Fields left the Old Corner, selling their lease and the good-will of the retail business to E. P. Dutton & Co. which later became a famous New York house. After a few years Ticknor & Fields became Fields, Osgood & Co., then James R. Osgood & Co., and finally, by consolidation, Houghton, Mifflin & Co.

The original Houghton, Henry O., was a Vermonter, a printer's devil in Burlington at thirteen who worked his way through the local college and came to Boston as a type-setter and reporter on the 'Traveller' at five dollars a week. His type-setting only occupied ten hours of his day, after which he was free for reporting. He could write out a sermon or a lecture from memory. Presently, on a shoestring, he bought himself into the printing firm which became Bolles & Houghton; and so was on his way to the headship of the firm of H. O. Houghton & Co. and its Riverside Press. A street near the plant of that famous press had been named for the earliest colonial printer, Stephen Daye. So the art of printing, in America, came to its fine flowering in the place where the seed was dropped.

Other great names in American publishing tempt me, but they are mostly beyond the range of this record. One Philadelphia house still bears the name of its founder. J. B. Lippincott, after due experience as clerk and manager for others, set up his own bookshop in 1836. He began at once to publish books under the imprint of J. B. Lippincott & Co.

The Boston Renaissance 195

He specialized in finely bound Bibles, prayer books, and gift-books. His career as a publisher was broadened when he acquired the rights in Prescott's works, in 1857; and from that time on the Lippincotts took their place among the leading general publishers of the country. Meanwhile the Careys had passed their prime. Philadelphia had lapsed to a bad third as a publishing centre. Boston was for the time being in the ascendant. New York's later, and as it now seems permanent, conquest of the field was still some distance in the future.

So we have reached and perhaps slipped past the mark set for this chronicle. The decade centering in 1850 was a turning point in many ways. It marked the end of the first placid and unchallenged phase of capitalist rule. It marked a feverish heightening of those diverse forces which were breeding the panic of '57 and the War of the Rebellion. And it marked with extraordinary clearness the birth of modern literature. It produced 'Jane Eyre' and 'The Scarlet Letter,' 'Vanity Fair' and 'Walden,' the 'Biglow Papers' and 'Uncle Tom.' It marked, we may say, the emergence of modern publishing, with its centralization and specialization, its improved ethics, and, alas! its submergence of the homely or picturesque aspects of bookselling in the older time.

SOURCE BOOKS

ADAMS, J. T. *Provincial Society, 1690-1783.* New York, 1927.*
The Epic of America. Boston, 1931.†
ADKINS, N. F. *Fitz-Greene Halleck: An Early Knickerbocker Wit and Poet.* New Haven, 1930.
BIBLIOGRAPHICAL ESSAYS: *A Tribute to Wilberforce Eames.* Edited by G. P. Winship and L. C. Wroth. Cambridge, 1924.
BRADFORD, W. *The History of Plymouth Plantation.* Boston, 1898.
BRADSHER, E. L. *Mathew Carey, Editor, Author, and Publisher.* New York, 1912.‡
Book Publishers and Publishing. The Cambridge History of American Literature. Vol. IV. New York, 1921.
CHAPLIN, J. *The Life of Henry Dunster.* Boston, 1872.
COOPER, J. F., Ed. *Correspondence of James Fenimore Cooper.* New Haven, 1922.
COOPER, S. *Pages and Pictures from the Writings of James Fenimore Cooper.* New York, 1861.
DERBY, J. C. *Fifty Years Among Authors, Books and Publishers.* New York, 1884.
DUNTON, J. *The Life and Errors of John Dunton.* London, 1705. Reprinted 1818.
EAMES, W. *The Bay Psalm Book.* New York, 1903.
The First Year of Printing in New York. New York, 1928.
EDDY, G. C. *Account Books Kept by Benjamin Franklin.* New York, 1928, 1929.

* Excerpts quoted by permission of The Macmillan Co.
† Excerpts quoted by permission of Little, Brown & Co.
‡ Excerpts quoted by permission of the Columbia University Press.

Source Books

EVANS, C. W. *American Bibliography, 1639-1796.* Chicago, 1903-1929. 10 Vols.
FORD, P. L. *Journals of Hugh Gaine, Printer.* New York, 1902.
The New England Primer, New York, 1897.
FORD, W. C. *The Boston Book Market, 1697-1700.* Boston, 1917.
FRANCIS, J. *Old New York.* New York, 1865.
FRANKLIN, B. *Autobiography.* Philadelphia, 1868.
GREEN, J. R. *A Short History of the English People.* London, 1874.
GREEN, S. A. *John Foster, The Earliest American Engraver and the First Boston Printer.* Boston, 1909.
HARPER, J. H. *The House of Harper.* New York, 1912.
HELLMAN, G., Ed. *Letters of Henry Brevoort to Washington Irving.* New York, 1916.
Letters of Washington Irving to Henry Brevoort. New York, 1915.
HILDEBURN, C. R. *A List of the Issues of the Press in New York, 1693-1752.* Philadelphia, 1889.
Sketches of Printers and Printing in Early New York. New York, 1912.
IRVING, P. *The Life and Letters of Washington Irving.* New York, 1864.
KNIGHT, C. *Shadows of the Old Booksellers.* London, 1865.
LITTLEFIELD, G. E. *Early Boston Booksellers, 1642-1711.* Boston, 1900.
The Early Massachusetts Press, 1638-1711.
MANN, C. L. *A Century of Bookselling: The Story of the Old Corner Book Store.* Boston, 1928.
MUMBY, F. A. *The Romance of Bookselling.* London, 1910.
Publishing and Bookselling, New York, 1931.
NICHOLS, C. L. *Isaiah Thomas, Printer, Writer and Collector.* Boston, 1912.
OBERHOLTZER, E. P. *The Literary History of Philadelphia.* Philadelphia, 1906.

ONE HUNDRED YEARS OF PUBLISHING: *A Brief Historical Account of the History of William Wood & Co.* New York, 1904.

OVERTON, G. *Portrait of a Publisher: The First Hundred Years of the House of Appleton, 1825-1925.* New York, 1925.

PARRINGTON, V. L. *The Colonial Mind, 1620-1800.* New York, 1927.

PAULDING, W. *The Literary Life of James K. Paulding.* New York, 1867.

PUTNAM, G. H. *George Palmer Putnam: A Memoir.* New York, 1912.
Memories of a Publisher. New York, 1915.

PUTNAM, G. P. *American Facts: Notes and Statistics, etc.* London, 1845.

RODEN, R. F. *The Cambridge Press, 1638-1692.* New York, 1915.

RUTHERFURD, L. *John Peter Zenger: His Trial, etc.* New York, 1904.

SEWALL, S. *Diary of Samuel Sewall.* Boston, 1878.

SKEEL, E. E. F. *Mason Locke Weems, His Works and Ways.* Vol. I. Bibliography; Vols. II and III, Letters. New York, 1929.

TICKNOR, C. *Hawthorne and His Publisher.* Boston, 1913.

THOMAS, I. *A History of Printing.* Worcester, 1910. Reprinted Albany, 1874.

WENDELL, B. *A Literary History of America.* New York, 1901.

WHITCOMB, S. L. *Chronological Outlines of American Literature.* New York, 1894.

WRIGHT, T. G. *The Literary Culture of Early New England.* New Haven, 1920.

WROTH, L. C. *Parson Weems.* Baltimore, 1911.
William Goddard and Some of His Friends. R. I. Historical Society, 1924.
The Colonial Printer. New York, 1931.

INDEX

A

'Abbot,' 24
'Account of the Discovery,' etc., Buckland's, 26
Adams, James Truslow, 29, 98
Addison, Joseph, 52, 110, 127
'Advancement of Learning,' 25
Advertising, 66
Aesop, 36
Aiken, Robert, 136
à Kempis, Thomas, 37
Albany, 16, 121
Aldrich, Thomas Bailey, 179
Allen, John, 192
Allen & Ticknor, 167, 191
Almanacs, 47, 54, 79, 102
Americana, 122, 130
American Antiquarian Society, 122
American Company of Booksellers, 137, 138
'American Facts,' etc., 171
'American Magazine,' Rogers & Fowle's, 81
American magazines, 102, 127, 148
'American Museum,' Carey's, 129, 130
American publishing, phases of, 123, 124, 125, 127, 137, 138-140, 144, 153, 154, 157, 178
Ames's 'Almanack,' 124
Andover, Mass., 169, 180
Andros, Sir Edmund, 43
'Animated Nature,' 135

Annapolis, 88
Anne, Queen, 52
'Appeal to Common Sense,' M. Carey's, 150
'Appeal to the Wealthy,' M. Carey's, 150
Appleton, Daniel, 167, 180
Appleton, William H., 180, 181
Appleton & Co., D., 181
Appletons, 83, 149, 154, 180-182
'Arcadia,' Sidney's, 11, 36
Arnold, Benedict, bookseller, 101
'Arthur Mervyn,' Brockden Brown's, 149
'Art of Love,' Ovid's, 36
'Athenian Mercury,' Dunton's, 47
Austen, Jane, 139
Autobiographical fragment, G. P. Putnam's, 167-169
'Autobiography,' Franklin's, 71, 75

B

Bache, Benjamin Franklin, 77, 78
Bacon, Lord, 5, 14, 36
Baird, Henry Carey, 150, 179
Baltimore press, 83, 85, 155
Bank of the United States, 150
Barlow, Joel, 122
Barrett, Elizabeth, 172
Bartlett, John, 189
'Baskerville of America,' 122
Battelle, Ebenezer, 188
'Bay Psalm Book,' 23, 27, 28, 31

'Bibliophobia,' 169
'Biglow Papers,' 195
Blackstone, Sir William, 137
Blake, W. P. & L., 188
Blanchard & Lea, 149
Bleecker, G. W., 166
'Bloody Tenent,' Williams's, 29
Bolles & Houghton, 194
Book collectors, 42, 138
'Book fairs,' German, 25
'Book of Knowledge,' Thomas's, 118
Book piracy, 141, 146, 163
Booksellers and colonial culture, 6, 7, 35, 98, 99, 137
Booksellers' exchange, 46, 137
Bookselling in Rome, 1, 46
Boston, 27, 152, 188-194
Boston booksellers, 32, 35, 36-38, 47-51, 81
Boston fire of 1711, 51, 52
'Boston News-Letter,' 67
Boston press, 32, 41-43
Boulter, 35
'Bracebridge Hall,' 159
Bradford, Andrew, 58, 62, 71, 73, 114, 115
Bradford, Governor William, 25
Bradford, Thomas, 116
Bradford, William, printer, 31, 54-64, 71, 76, 81, 82, 84, 94, 98
Bradford, William, 3rd, 114
Bradfords, 83
Bradsher, E. L., 136, 148
Bradstreet, Anne, 4
Bread and Cheese Club, 163
Bremer, Frederika, 186
Brevoort, Henry, 153, 158, 159
Brewster, Elder William, 18, 25
Briggs, Charles F., 177, 178
Brimmer, George W., 191

British Museum, 6
British provincial presses, 28, 29, 31
Brooker, William, 68
Brookfield, Mass., 121
Brooklyn, Battle of, 105
Brown, Charles Brockden, 126
Brown, James, 88, 170
Brown, William, 142
Browne, Sir Thomas, 26
Browning, Robert, 173
Brunning, Joseph, 46
Bryan, Hugh, 89
Bryant, William Cullen, 126, 147, 163, 181, 184
Buckingham, Duke of, 15
Buckland, James, 126
Budd, Thomas, 115
Bulwer, Edward, 143, 148, 183
Bunyan, John, 14, 52
Byron, Lord, 139, 140

C

Calvin, John, 5
Cambridge, Mass., 19, 23
Cambridge press, 7, 13, 20-24, 28, 32, 37
Cambridge University, 22, 23
Camden, William, 26
Campbell, John, 67, 68
Campbell, Thomas, 172
Carey, Baird & Co., 149
Carey, Edward L., 149
Carey, Henry C., 148, 150, 151
Carey, Lea & Blanchard, 149
Carey, Lea & Carey, 149
Carey, Matthew, 125, 127-138, 140, 148, 149-151, 156
Carey & Hart, 143, 149
Carey & Lea, 142, 148, 164, 168

INDEX 201

Careys, 144, 147, 164, 181
Carlyle, Thomas, 173, 174
Carter, John, 87
Carter, Timothy, 190-192
Carter & Hendee, 189-192
Carvill, G. & C., 168
'Cato,' Addison's, 110
'Censor,' Russell's, 117
Censorship and licensing of the press, 7, 41, 56, 90, 95, 96
Charles II, King, 14, 27
Charleston, 83, 88, 90
Charlestown, 43, 121
'Charlotte Temple,' 139
'Cheshire Advertiser,' 61
Chiswell, Richard, 35, 111
Church of England, 5, 18, 104, 132
Cicero, 77
College of New Jersey (Princeton), 54
Collins, J. B., 168
Collins, Wilkie, 186
Colonial clubs, 53, 102
Colonial culture, 27, 64, 102
Colonial magazines, 54, 65, 102
Colonial newspapers, 48, 49, 52, 54, 65-70
Colonial scholarship, 18, 19, 26, 34
'Columbian Magazine,' 129
'Common Sense,' Paine's, 105
'Complete System of Arithmetic,' Pike's, 124
Concord, Mass., 121
'Confessions,' Simms's, 147
'Congratulation,' Odell's, 112
Congreve, William, 52
'Connecticut Gazette,' Holt's, 100
Constable (publisher), 140, 149
Constitutional Post Office, 86
Continental Army, 105, 106
Continental Congress, 86

Cook, Judge, 57
Copley, John Singleton, 102
Copyright, 12, 146, 170, 172, 178, 179, 185, 186
Cotton, John, 4, 29, 40, 45, 53
Cowley, Abraham, 15
Crease, Thomas, 189
'Crisis,' M. Carey's, 150
'Croaker Papers,' 158
Crocker & Brewster, 167
Cromwell, Oliver, 27
Crosby, Governor, 95
Cummings & Hilliard, 167
Cupples & Upham, 191
Cut-throat publishing, 139-148, 163, 186

D

Damrell & Upham, 189
Dana, Richard Henry, 163
Danter, 12
Darwin, Charles, 181
'Day of Doom,' Wigglesworth's, 28
Daye, Matthew, 24
Daye, Stephen, 21, 23, 24, 27, 194
Dearborn, George, 168
Defoe, Daniel, 110, 123, 149
Dekker, Thomas, 25
Delancy, Abraham, 64
Denham, Sir John, 151
Derby, J. C., 142
Didot, François, 77, 128
Disraeli, Benjamin, 148
'Don Juan,' 140, 142
Drake, Joseph Rodman, 158
Draper, John, 124
Drayton, William Henry, 90, 91
Dryden, John, 14, 52, 110

Dueling, 128, 129, 156
'Dunciad,' 47
Dunster, Henry, 21-24, 36
Dunster, John, 21, 24
Dunton, John, 43-48, 50
Dutch American press, 97
Dutton, E. P. & Co., 191, 194
Duyckinck, E. A. & G. L., 168
Duyckinck, Evert, 168
Dwight, Timothy, 126, 127
'Dying Groans,' Dunton's, 48

E

'Early Boston Booksellers,' 51
Edes & Gill, 116
Editions, issues, printings, impressions, 172 note
Edwards, Jonathan, 53
Eliot, John, 27, 29, 30, 31
Elizabeth, Queen, 3, 5, 11
Elizabethan period, 3, 4
Emerson, Ralph Waldo, 127, 174, 192
'Essays on Political Economy,' M. Carey's, 150
'Essays on the Rates of Wages,' M. Carey's, 150
Etheredge, Sir George, 52
'Euterpiad,' Bleecker's, 166
Evacuation of New York, 107
'Evening Post,' Boston, 66
'Everyman's Library,' 184

F

'Fable for Critics,' 177
'Fanny,' Halleck's, 157, 158, 161, 184
Federalists, 129

Field, Cyrus, 179
Fields, James T., 193
Fields, Osgood & Co., 194
Fleet, T. & J., 124
Fleet, Thomas, 65, 66, 118
Fleet Street, 7
Ford, Worthington C., 61
Foster, John, 38-41
Fowle, Daniel, 81, 82
Fowle, Zechariah, 82, 118, 119
Franklin, Anne, 78, 79
Franklin, Benjamin, 38, 53, 58, 62, 70-76, 87, 88, 98, 122, 128, 130, 131
Franklin, James, 67-70, 72, 73, 78, 79, 83, 98
Franklin, James, Jr., 79
Franklin & Hall, 77
French American press, 97
French and Indian wars, 104
Freneau, Philip, 107, 109, 112, 126, 130, 147
'Friend of Peace,' Wood's, 154

G

Gaine, Hugh, 101-111, 127, 137
Galileo, 27
Gay, John, 61, 110
'General Gage's Confession,' Freneau's, 109
George Eliot, 186
George III, King, 156
German American press, 92-94, 97
German immigration, 92-93
Germantown, 58, 62, 94
Gillet, Jacob, 157
Girard, Stephen, 149
Glover, Jesse, 20-24
Glover, John, 21, 24

INDEX

Glover, Mrs. Jesse, 21
Goddard, Mary Katherine, 85-88
Goddard, Sarah, 84-87
Goddard, William, 84-87, 99
Goddards, 83
'Goddard's Post Office,' 86
Godwin, William, 126
Goldsmith, Oliver, 135
Goodrich, S. G., 191
'Goody Twoshoes,' 127
'Grammatical Institute,' Webster's, 125
'Grave,' Blair's, 110
'Great Expectations,' 186
Green, Bartholomew, 37, 124
Green, Samuel, 29, 31
Green, Samuel the younger, 42, 43
Green & Russell, 124
Greens, 83
Gridley, 65
'Guardian,' 68

H

Hakluyt, 25
Halifax, Lord, 48
'Halifax Gazette,' 118, 119
Hall, David, 77
Hall, Samuel, 79, 80
Hallams, 102
Halleck, Fitz-Greene, 127, 158, 163, 184
Halsteds, 161
Hamilton, Alexander, 156
Hamilton, Andrew, 95, 96
Harper, Fletcher, 187
Harper, J. & J., 157, 168, 183
Harper, J. Henry, 186
Harper, James, 182, 183
Harper, John, 184, 185

Harper, Joseph Wesley, 185
Harper & Brothers, 184
Harpers, 83, 123, 142, 143, 149, 154, 157, 164, 179, 182-187
Harris, Benjamin, 48-50
Hart, Abraham, 149
Harte, Bret, 179
Hartford Wits, 127, 130
Harvard, John, 19
Harvard College, 19-23, 30, 32
Harvard library, 19, 24, 34, 35, 41, 45
Hell-Fire Club, 69
Herbert, George, 36
Herbert of Cherbury, 27
Hilliard, Gray & Co., 167, 188
'History of New York,' Irving's, 153
'History of Plymouth,' Bradford's, 25
'History of Printing,' Thomas's, 39, 46, 121, 123
'History of the World,' Raleigh's, 25
'Histrio-Mastix,' Prynne's, 13
Holmes, Oliver Wendell, 192
Holt, Henry, 186
Holt, John, 100, 101
Hopkinson, Francis, 126, 130
Horace, 37
Houghton, Henry O., 194
Houghton, Mifflin & Co., 194
Howells, William Dean, 179
'Hudibras,' 68, 127
Huguenot culture, 97
Hutchinson, Governor, 120
Huxley, Thomas H., 181
'Hymns and Songs of the Church,' Wither's, 8

204   INDEX

I

'Imitatio Christi,' 37
'Independent Advertiser,' Rogers & Fowle's, 81
'Independent Gazetteer,' Oswald's, 129
Indians in New England, 29-31, 34
Inskeep & Bradford, 153
Irving, Pierre, 159
Irving, Washington, 127, 144, 152-154, 184
Irving - Brevoort correspondence, 154
'Isle of Pines,' 37
'Ivanhoe,' 24

J

James, Henry, 179
James I, King, 5, 8
James R. Osgood & Co., 194
'Jane Eyre,' 195
Jansen, 58, 62
'John Foster,' Green's, 38
John of London, 20, 24
Johnson, Marmaduke, 29-31, 32, 37
Johnson, Moses, 61
Johnson, Samuel, 6, 127
'Journal of the Plague Year,' Defoe's, 149
Juvenal, 37

K

'Kalendarium Pennsylvaniense,' 54
Keimer, Samuel, 74-76
Keith, George, 55
Keith, Governor William, 74
Kneeland, Daniel, 124
Kneeland, John, 125

Kneeland, Samuel, 69
Knight, Charles, 5, 6

L

Lafayette, Marquis de, 128
Lancaster, Pa., 145
'Last of the Mohicans,' 164
Lea, Henry C., 149
Lea, Isaac, 148
Lea & Blanchard, 146, 149
Lea Brothers & Co., 149
'Leatherstocking Tales,' 147
Leavitt, Jonathan, 167, 168, 180
Lee, Samuel, 36
'Letter to His Countrymen,' Cooper's, 165
Lexington, Battle of, 120, 121
Lexington, Ky., 145
'Library of American Books,' 174, 177
'Library of Select Novels,' 185
'Life and Errors,' Dunton's, 43, 47
'Life of Byron,' Moore's, 144
'Life of Cromwell,' Carlyle's, 174
'Life of Irving,' 159
'Life of Washington,' Sparks's, 188
'Life of Washington,' Weems's, 135
'Life of Wellington,' 157
Lily, Wait & Co., 167
Lincoln, Governor, 122
Lincoln & Edwards, 167
Lintott, Bernard, 1
'Lionel Lincoln,' 164
Lippincott, J. B., 194
'Literary History of America,' Wendell's, 3
Literature and the book trade in seventeenth century England, 4-6
Little, Brown & Co., 188, 189
Little, Charles C., 188

INDEX 205

Little & Brown, 167, 170, 174
Livingston, Governor, 105
Locke, John, 72, 110
Long, George, 165
Longfellow, Henry Wadsworth, 193
Long Parliament, 13
Longworth, David, 152
Lowell, James Russell, 177, 178, 192

M

MacComb, John, 56
McElrath, Thomas, 142
McElrath & Bangs, 142
'McFingal,' Trumbull's, 130
Machiavelli, Niccolo, 25
Macmillan Co., 176
Mamaroneck, 160
Marryatt, Captain, 148
Maryland and German immigration, 93
'Maryland Journal,' Goddard's, 86, 87
Maryland manners, 132
Massachusetts Bay Colony, 5, 13, 18, 20, 27, 34
Massachusetts Bay Company, 18, 20
Massachusetts General Court, 19, 20, 22, 31, 38, 41
'Massachusetts Spy,' Thomas's, 119
Mather, Cotton, 22, 36, 42, 46, 71
Mather, Increase, 36, 39, 46, 69
Mather, Richard, 27
Mathers, 4, 38, 45, 48, 53, 68
'Medical Record,' 155
Melville, Herman, 174
Meredith, Hugh, 75
Merriams, 169
'Military Collections and Remarks,' 107

Miller, John, 141
Milton, John, 3, 14, 26, 27, 36, 55, 66, 123
'Modern Library,' 184
Mohawk prayer book, 31
'Monster of Monsters,' 81
Moore, Thomas, 141
'Morals,' Seneca's, 183, 187
Morse, Jedediah, 124
Morse, S. F. B., 163
'Mosses from an Old Manse,' 174
Mount Vernon, 128
Mumby, Frank A., 13
Murray, John, 182
'Mysteries of Udolpho,' 139

N

Nationalism and American books, 124, 126, 127
'Necker on Religion,' 130
Negroes advertised, 66, 110
Newark, N. J., 105
Newbery, John, 127
New Brunswick, 94
New Brunswick 'Royal Gazette,' 94
New England, 5, 7, 30, 34, 35, 54
'New England Courant,' J. Franklin's, 67-70, 78
'New England Primer,' 118
New Hampshire, 35, 43
New Hampshire press, 82
New Haven, 83, 99
New Jersey press, 99
Newport, 78, 79
'Newport Mercury,' 79, 80, 84
Newton, Sir Isaac, 16, 27
Newtown, Mass., 19
New York, illiteracy of, 34, 35, 64, 152

206 INDEX

'New York Gazette,' Bradford's, 63, 95
'New York Gazette,' Parker's, 101, 104
'New York Gazetteer,' Rivington's, 111
'New York Journal,' Holt's, 101
'New York Mercury,' Gaine's, 103, 104
New York press, 54, 58
New York 'Weekly Journal,' Zenger's, 94, 95
'New York Weekly Post-Boy,' Parker's, 99
'Night Thoughts,' 123
Norfolk press, 101
'Northanger Abbey,' 139
Nova Scotia press, 118
Novel, rise of, 126, 127, 139-144, 146

O

Odell, Jonathan, 112
Old Corner Book Store, 48, 163, 189-194
Old South Church, Boston, 32
'Olive Branch,' M. Carey's, 150
Osborn & Buckingham, 165
Oswald, Colonel, 129, 156.
Ovid, 36, 37
Oxford, 16, 22, 23
Oxford Society, 14

P

Paine, Thomas, 145
Pamphleteering, 6, 29, 102, 123
Paper making, 58-62, 88
'Paradise Lost,' 26
Parker, James, 84, 99, 100, 103

Parks, William, 88
Parrington, Vernon L., 3, 4, 16
'Parson Weems,' 131
Passy, Franklin at, 128
Paternoster Row, 170
Paulding, James K., 152, 153, 163
Penn, William, 35, 54, 57
Pennsylvania and German immigration, 93
'Pennsylvania Chronicle,' Goddard's, 85
'Pennsylvania Gazette,' Franklin's, 77
'Pennsylvania Herald,' Carey's, 129
Pennsylvania press, 7, 54, 63
Pepys, Samuel, 42
Percival, James G., 163
'Peveril of the Peak,' 141
Philadelphia, 54-58, 64, 71, 129, 152
Phillips, Samuel, 48, 50
'Pickwick Papers,' 45
'Picturesque America,' Bryant's, 181
'Pilot,' 164
'Pioneers,' 160
Plautus, 36
Plymouth Colony, 5, 17, 18, 25
Poe, Edgar Allan, 147, 151
'Poor Richard,' 73, 77, 79, 182
'Poor Robin,' 79
Pope, Alexander, 1, 52, 61, 110, 123
Porter, the Misses, 184
Portsmouth, N. H., 145
Post-Revolutionary magazines, 127, 128
Post-Revolutionary newspapers, 128
Powell, Thomas, 90-92
'Precaution,' 160
Presbyterians in New York, 104
Prescott, William H., 195

INDEX

Prince Rupert, 27
'Prospects on and beyond the Rubicon,' M. Carey's, 150
Providence, 83
'Providence Gazette,' Goddard's, 84, 87
'Provincial Society,' Adams's, 53
Prynne, William, 13
'Psalm Book in Meter,' 8
Public libraries, 35, 102
'Public Occurrences,' Harris's, 48
Publishing methods, 1, 2, 8, 9, 83, 124-126, 131, 140-146
Puritan attitude toward literature, 3, 16, 36, 37, 71
Puritan scholarship, 18, 23, 83
Puritan theocracy, 18, 19, 21
Putnam, George Haven, 138, 174, 186
Putnam, George Palmer, 166, 167, 169, 174, 178
Putnams, 83, 154

Q

Quakers, 54, 57, 58
'Quentin Durward,' 141

R

Reading, Pa., 145
Reed, John, 193
'Refuge in Time of Plague,' Appleton's, 181
Regicides, 26
Renaissance, Italian, 4
Restoration, 14, 26, 52
Revere, Paul, 120
Revolution, War of, 7, 59, 62, 80, 90, 94, 102, 105, 114-120
Rhode Island press, 78, 80, 84

Richardson, Samuel, 110
'Rienzi,' Bulwer's, 143
Riverside Press, 194
Rivington, James, 101, 102, 105, 108, 110-113
'Rivington's Confessions,' 112
'Robinson Crusoe,' 61
Rochester, Earl of, 52
Rogers, Gamaliel, 81
'Romeo and Juliet,' 12
'Rory O'More,' Lover's, 138
'Royal Gazette,' Rivington's, 111, 112
Royal Society, 14-16, 37
Royalists, Tories, 85, 102, 106, 107, 111, 117, 120, 123, 127
Royalty payment, 2, 172
Ruskin, John, 175
Russell, Ezekiel, 117
Rutherfurd, Livingston, 96

S

St. Mery, Moreau, 97
St. Paul's Churchyard, 7, 11, 29, 35, 51
'Saint's Rest,' Baxter's, 123
Salem, 45, 79
'Salmagundi,' 152, 153, 155, 158
Sandwich Islands, 172
'Scarlet Letter,' 193, 195
'Scholler's Purgatory,' 8-11
Scotch-Irish immigration, 103
Scott, Sir Walter, 139, 148, 184
'Scurriliad,' M. Carey's, 129
'Seaside Library,' Harpers', 185
Sewall, Samuel, 41, 42, 48
Shaftesbury, Earl of, 72
Shakespeare, William, 1, 16
Shepard, Thomas, 36
'Short Account,' M. Carey's, 149

208 INDEX

Sidney, Sir Philip, 11, 36
Simms, William Gilmore, 147
Sinclair, Upton, 175
'Sketch Book,' 153, 158, 159, 162
Small town printing, 145
Smith, Adam, 137, 150
Smith, John, 16
Smith, Sydney, 171
Society for the Propagation of the Gospel, 29, 30, 32
Socratic method, 72
South Carolina, 119
'South Carolina Gazette,' Timothy's, 88, 89
Southern culture, 61
Southwick, Solomon, 80
Sowers, Christopher, 93, 94
Specialization in publishing, 2, 144, 155, 175, 176
'Spectator,' 65, 68, 69
Spencer, Herbert, 181
Stamp Act, 104, 115, 116, 119
Star Chamber, 13
Stationers' Company, 1, 8, 11, 12, 13, 137
Stationers' Register, 13
Stereotyping, 138
Sterne, Laurence, 123
Sternhold and Hopkins, 27
Swift, Jonathan, 48, 52
Swords, T. & T., 168

T

'Tale of a Tub,' 68
'Tales,' Poe's (1845), 174
'Tales of the Grotesque and Arabesque,' 147
Tate and Brady, 28
'Tatler,' 152
Temple, Sir William, 48

Thackeray, William Makepeace, 148, 186
Thirty Years' War, 93
Thomas, Isaiah, 38, 40, 44, 45, 47, 72, 75, 76, 80, 84, 90, 114, 115-122, 124, 130
Thomas, Isaiah, Jr., 121
Thomas, Moses, 159
Thomas & Fowle, 118
Thomson, James, 110, 123
Ticknor, Reed & Fields, 193
Ticknor, William D., 192-193
Ticknor & Fields, 167, 193-194
Timothy, Anne, 90
Timothy, Benjamin Franklin, 90
Timothy, Lewis (Louis Timothée), 88-90
Timothy, Peter, 88-90
'Titus Andronicus,' 12
Town House, Boston, 35, 51
Trenton, Battle of, 115
Trinity Church, New York, 155
Trollope, Anthony, 186
Trumbull, John, 126, 127, 130
Tyndall, John, 181
'Typee,' 174

U

'Uncle Tom's Cabin,' 195
Usher, Hezekiah, 32, 38, 43
Usher, John, 32, 33, 35, 36, 43

V

Van Dam, Kip, 95
'Vanity Fair,' 195
Van Winkle, C. S., 157-159
Van Winkle & Wiley, 157
Verplanck, Gulian C., 163
Virginia, 5, 7, 31

INDEX

'Virginia Gazette,' Parker's, Parks's, 61, 68
'Virginians,' 186
'Volunteer's Journal,' 128

W

'Walden,' 195
Waller, Edmund, 14
Walpole, N. H., 121
Walton, Isaac, 14
War of 1812, 150
Ward, Nathaniel, 4
Wardle, Thomas, 164
Washington, George, 105, 106, 107, 130, 132
Waterloo Place, 171
Watertown, Mass., 116
Watts's 'Hymns', 61, 110
'Waverley Novels,' 140, 144, 161
Webster, Noah, 124, 125, 126, 130
Weed, Thurlow, 182
'Weekly Rehearsal,' 65
Weems, Mason Locke, 131-136, 138
West, Benjamin, 102
Whigs, 80, 85, 86, 101, 106, 111, 119, 156
Whitefield, George, 89
Whittier, John Greenleaf, 192, 193
'Whole Booke of Psalmes,' 27
'Wieland,' 126
Wigglesworth, Michael, 28
Wiley, Charles, 48, 144, 155-164
Wiley, John, 155, 156, 159, 164, 165, 174
Wiley, John, & Sons, 175
Wiley, Major John, 155
Wiley & Halsted, 161
Wiley & Long, 165, 166
Wiley & Putnam, 166-175, 193
Wileys, 154
Wilkins, Richard, 48
William and Mary College, 54
Williams, R. P. & C., 167
Williams, Roger, 4, 26, 29, 78
Williamsburg, 88, 100
Winthrop, John, 19, 36
Winthrops, 25, 26
Witch-hanging, 32, 42
Wither, George, 7-11, 25
Witherspoon, Rev. Mr., 113
Wood, William & Co., 154-155
Woodbridge, Benjamin, 40
Worcester, 121
Wotton, Sir Henry, 27
Wren, Sir Christopher, 27
Wright, T. G., 25, 26, 28
Wroth, L. C., 60, 87, 136
Wycherley, William, 52

Y

Yale College, 54
Youmans, Edward L., 181
Young, Edward, 110

Z

Zenger, Catherine, 96
Zenger, John Peter, 94-96
Zenger, John Peter, Jr., 96